Conferderate Poets
Volume II

Portraits:

Top Left: Abram J. Ryan

Top Right: Daniel B. Lucas

Center: Innes Randolph

Bottom Left: Paul H. Hayne

Bottom Right: Henry T. Stanton

The Land They Loved:
Volume III

CONFEDERATE
Poets & Poems
Volume II

Edited by
Clyde N. Wilson

CONTENTS

No people has ever existed wholly without a meaning.

—James Warley Miles, Charleston sermon, 1863

FOREWORD

THIS IS THE THIRD in a six-volume series intended to tell the history of the Southern people in verse in the certainty that poets sometimes convey a kind of truth not necessarily evident in other records. Thus, literary merit is not the first consideration here, although some of the material has much long-unrecognised merit. This merit is likely to remain unrecognised if not entirely lost as historical amnesia and the gutting of cultural standards mark our ongoing decline in Western civilisation. Especially since the South, without doubt the most important "diversity" in American history, is exiled from the dominant official "multiculturalism."

This is the second volume to present the Southern mind and soul in the great catastrophe of the War for Southern Independence. The folklorist Richard Chase has written, truly:

> It is only when our old songs and old tales are passing from one human being to another, by word-of-mouth that they can attain their full fascination. No printed page can create this spell. It is the living word—the sung ballad and the told tale—that holds our attention and reaches our hearts.

Though we cannot provide music we have generously included song lyrics that show the Southern spirit. Where the author of the lyrics is known they will be found under the author's name, otherwise standing alone. Sometimes words and songs were written together. At other times popular verses were set to familiar music. "Maryland, My Maryland" was sung to the notes of "Tannenbaum" and "For Bales" to those of the Yankee "When Johnny Comes Marching Home." Many lyrics have no certain authors or publishers and have been collected from folk sources. We have generally included songs of certain Southern origin. Many of the most familiar songs were popular on both sides like the Northern-born "All Quiet along the Potomac" and "Lorena" and the Southern "Somebody's Darling." An interesting fact of the War is that bands just behind the front lines sometimes serenaded the other side.

Union poems and song lyrics during the war tended toward militant self-righteousness or Victorian sentimentality: "The Battle Hymn of the Republic" and "We are Coming Father Abraham." As Sidney Lanier wrote of Walt Whitman: "As near as I can make it out, Whitman's argument seems to be, that because a prairie is wide, therefore debauchery is admirable, and because the Mississippi is long, therefore every American is God."

Confederates, when not serious generally produced rollicking, high spirited words in music like "Jine the Calvary." It is conventional that Southern culture was romantic. Contrarily, Southern poets often show their classical education. The absolutely and marvelously definitive presentation of Confederate songs has been made by Bobby Horton of Alabama and his recordings of "Homespun Songs of the CSA." May his work have a long life.

Remember that no large group of Americans has fought so bravely and skillfully, with such dedication, sacrifice, and suffering. That should be kept in mind while reading those who expressed themselves in verse under the highest hopes, severest trials, and deepest losses.

Studying these verses will establish beyond a doubt that Confederates were learned and thoughtful people, and that the Lost Cause was a great deal more than a Myth.

Clyde Wilson

Dutch Fork, South Carolina

I. Trial By Fire

Men who saw night coming down about them could somehow act as if they stood at the edge of dawn.

—Stone Mountain Inscription

JAMES RUSSELL BARRICK (1829—1867) was a native of Kentucky and was at one time the editor of the *Atlanta Constitution*.

Kentucky, She is Sold

A tear for "the dark and bloody ground,"
For the land of hills and caves;
Her Kentons, Boones, and her Shelbys sleep
Where the vandals tread their graves;
A sigh for the loss of her honoured fame,
Dear won in the days of old;
Her ship is manned by a foreign crew,
For Kentucky, she is sold.

The bones of her sons lie bleaching on
The plains of Tippecanoe,
On the field of Raisin her blood was shed,
As free as the summer's dew;
In Mexico her McRee and Clay
Were first of the brave and bold—
A change has been in her bosom wrought,
For Kentucky, she is sold.

Pride of the free, was that noble State,
And her banner still were so,
Had the iron heel of the despot not
Her prowess sunk so low;
Her valleys once were the freeman's home,
Her valour unbought with gold,
But now the pride of her life is fled,
For Kentucky, she is sold

Her brave would once have scorned to wear
The yoke that crushes her now,
And the tyrant grasp, and the vandal tread,
Would sullen have made her brow;
Her spirit yet will be wakened up,
And her saddened fate be told,
Her gallant sons to the world yet prove
That Kentucky is not sold.

♦ ♦ ♦

"BOONE"

Kentucky Required to Yield Her Arms

Ho! will the despot trifle,
    In dwellings of the free;
Kentuckians yield the rifle,
    Kentuckians bend the knee!
With dastard fear of danger,
    And trembling at the strife;
Kentucky, to the stranger,
    Yield liberty for life!
Up! up! each gallant ranger,
    With rifle and with knife!

The bastard and the traitor,
    The wolfcub and the snake,
The robber, swindler, hater,
    Are in your homes—awake!
Nor let the cunning foeman
    Despoil your liberty;
Yield weapon up to no man,
    While ye can strike and see,
Awake, each gallant yeoman,
    If still ye would be free!

Aye, see to sight the rifle,
    And smite with spear and knife,
Let no base cunning stifle
    Each lesson of your life:
How won your gallant sires
    The country which ye keep?
By soul, which still inspires
    The soil on which ye weep!
Leap up! their spirit fires,
    And rouse ye from your sleep!

"What!" cry the sires so famous,
    In Orleans' ancient field,
"Will ye, our children, shame us,
    And to the despot yield?
What! each brave lesson stifle
    We left to give you life?
Let apish despots trifle
    With home and child and wife?
And yield, O shame! the rifle,
    And sheathe, O shame! the knife?"

♦ ♦ ♦

"BULL RUN: A PARODY"

Bull Run: A Parody

At Bull Run when the sun was low,
Each Southern face grew pale as snow,
While loud as jackdaws rose the crow
Of Yankees boasting terribly!

But Bull Run saw another sight,
When at the deepening shades of night,
Towards Fairfax Court-House rose the flight
Of Yankees running rapidly.

Then broke each corps with terror riven,
Then rushed the steeds from battle driven,
The men of battery Number Seven
Forsook their Red artillery!

Still on McDowell's farthest left,
The roar of cannon strikes one deaf,
Where furious Abe and fiery Jeff
Contend for death or victory.
The panic thickens-off, ye brave!
Throw down your arms! your bacon save!
Waive, Washington, all scruples waive,
And fly, with all your chivalry!

♦ ♦ ♦

"CHEER, BOYS, CHEER."

Cheer, Boys, Cheer

Cheer, boys, cheer! We'll march away to battle!
Cheer, boys, cheer, for our sweethearts and our wives!
Cheer, boys, cheer! We'll nobly do our duty,
And give to the South our hearts, our arms, our lives.

Bring forth the flag, our country's noble standard;
Wave it on high till the wind shakes each fold out.
Proudly it floats, nobly waving in the vanguard;
Then cheer, boys, cheer! with a lusty, long, bold shout.

Cheer, boys, cheer! We'll march away to battle!
Cheer, boys, cheer, for our sweethearts and our wives!
Cheer, boys, cheer! We'll nobly do our duty,
And give to the South our hearts, our arms, our lives.

But as we march, with heads all lowly bending,
Let us implore a blessing from on high.
Our cause is just, the right we're defending,
And the God of battle will listen to our cry.

Cheer, boys, cheer! We'll march away to battle!
Cheer, boys, cheer, for our sweethearts and our wives!
Cheer, boys, cheer! We'll nobly do our duty,
And give to the South our hearts, our arms, our lives.

Tho' to the homes we never may return,
Ne'er press again our lov'd ones in our arms,
O'er our lone graves their faithful hearts will mourn,
Then cheer, boys, cheer! Such death hath no alarms.

Cheer, boys, cheer! We'll march away to battle!
Cheer, boys, cheer, for our sweethearts and our wives!
Cheer, boys, cheer! We'll nobly do our duty,
And give to the South our hearts, our arms, our lives.

♦ ♦ ♦

WALTER A. CLARK (1842–?) of Georgia was a Confederate Major, an uncollected poet, and the author of, among other works, *"Lost Arcadia, or the Story of Old Time Brothersville"* and *"Under the Stars and Bars or Memories of Four Years Service."* His theme here is of course the heroic South Carolina soldier Richard Kirkland who at Fredericksburg with great risk, tended the Yankee wounded left on the field. As far as may be determined, there is no Yankee Richard Kirkland. Kirkland was killed in action later in the war. (This poet is not to be confused with Walter Clark, the North Carolina Confederate officer and author.)

The Angel of Marye's Heights

A sunken road and a wall of stone
And Cobb's grim line of grey
Lay still at the base of Marye's hill
On the morn of a winter's day.

And crowning the frowning crest above
Sleep Alexander's guns,
While gleaming fair in the sunlit air
The Rappahannock runs.

On the plains below, the blue lines glow,
And the bugle rings out clear,
As with bated breath they march to death
And a soldier's honoured bier.

For the slumbering guns awake to life
And the screaming shell and ball
From the front and flanks crash through the ranks
And leave them where they fall.

And the grey stone wall is ringed with fire
And the pitiless leaden hail
Drives back the foe to the plains below,
Shattered and crippled and frail.

Again and again a new line forms
And the gallant charge is made,
And again and again they fall like grain
In the sweep of the reaper's blade.

And then from out of the battle smoke,
There falls on the lead swept air,
From the whitening lips that are ready to die
The piteous moan and the plaintive cry
For "Water" everywhere.

And into the presence of Kershaw brave,
There comes a fair faced lad,
With quivering lips, as his cap he tips,
"I can't stand this," he said.

"Stand what?" the general sternly said,
As he looked on the field of slaughter;
"To see those poor boys dying out there,
With no one to help them, no one to care
And crying for 'Water! Water!'

"If you'll let me go, I'll give them some."
"Why, boy, you're simply mad;
They'll kill you as soon as you scale the wall
In this terrible storm of shell and ball,"
The general kindly said.

"Please let me go," the lad replied.
"May the Lord protect you, then,"
And over the wall in the hissing air,
He carried comfort to grim despair,
And balm to the stricken men.

And as he straightened the mangled limbs
On their earthen bed of pain,
The whitening lips all eagerly quaffed
From the canteen's mouth the cooling draught
And blessed him again and again.

Like Daniel of old in the lions' den,
He walked through the murderous air,
With never a breath of the leaden storm
To touch or to tear his grey clad form,
For the hand of God was there.

And I am sure in the Book of Gold,
Where the blessèd Angel writes
The names that are blest of God and men,
He wrote that day with his shining pen,
Then smiled and lovingly wrote again
"The Angel of Marye's Heights."

♦ ♦ ♦

JOHN ESTEN COOKE (1830—1886) of Virginia was already a popular novelist before the War for Southern Independence. He served throughout the war, mainly on the staff of Gen. J.E.B. Stuart. His works include *Surry of Eagle's Nest, The Virginia Comedians, Wearing of the Gray, Outlines from the Outpost,* and biographies of Stuart and Lee. This poem was a response to the death of John Pelham.

The Band in the Pines

Oh, band in the pine-wood, cease!
Cease with your splendid call;
The living are brave and noble,
But the dead were bravest of all!

They throng to the martial summons,
To the loud triumphant strain;
And the dear, bright eyes of long dead friends
Come to the heart again.

They come with the ringing bugle,
And the deep drum's mellow roar,
Till the soul is faint with longing
For the hands we clasp no more.

Oh, band in the pine-wood, cease,
Or the heart will melt in tears,
For the gallant eyes and the smiling lips
And the voices of old years.

♦ ♦ ♦

"THE COTTON-BURNERS' HYMN." One of the primary activities of the U.S. Army during The War and of federal bureaucrats afterwards was seizing cotton which had risen in value due to the blockade of Southern ports. The proceeds were supposed to go to the Treasury but seldom did. Instead they made many Northerners rich. Southerners, on the other hand, destroyed their own property rather than let it fall to the enemy—including naval stores and rice as well as cotton. This verse was written in response to the burning of 800,000 bales of the cotton of West Tennessee and Mississippi, a three-day event reported in the Memphis Appeal.

The Cotton-Burners' Hymn

Lo! where Mississippi rolls

Oceanward its stream,

Upward mounting, folds on folds,

Flaming fire-tongues gleam;

"Tis the planters' grand oblation

On the altar of the nation;

'Tis a willing sacrifice—

Let the golden incense rise—

Pile the Cotton to the skies!

Lo! the sacrificial flame

Gilds the starry dome of night!

Nations! read the mute acclaim—

'Tis for liberty we fight!

Homes! Religion! Right!

Never such a golden light
Lit the vaulted sky;
Never sacrifice as bright,
Rose to God on high:
Thousands oxen, what were they
To the offering we pay?
And the brilliant holocaust—
When the revolution's past—
In the nation's songs will last!

Lo! the sacrificial flame
Gilds the starry dome of night!
Nations! read the mute acclaim—
'Tis for liberty we fight!
Homes! Religion! Right!

Though the night be dark above,
Broken though the shield—
Those who love us, those we love,
Bid us never yield:
Never! though our bravest bleed,
And the vultures on them feed;
Never! though the Serpents' race—
Hissing hate and vile disgrace—
By the million should menace!

Lo! the sacrificial flame
Gilds the starry dome of night!
Nations! read the mute acclaim—
'Tis for liberty we fight!
Homes! Religion! Right!

Pile the Cotton to the skies;
Lo! the Northmen gaze;
England! see our sacrifice
See the Cotton blaze!
God of nations! now to Thee,
Southrons bend th' imploring knee;
"Tis our country's hour of need—
Hear the mothers intercede
Hear the little children plead!

Lo! the sacrificial flame
Gilds the starry dome of night!
Nations! read the mute acclaim—
'Tis for liberty we fight!
Homes! Religion! Right!

◆ ◆ ◆

"CUMBERLAND GAP"

Cumberland Gap

The first white man in Cumberland Gap,
The first white man in Cumberland Gap.
The first white man in Cumberland Gap,
Was Doctor Walker, an English chap.
Lay down, boys and take a little nap.
They're raisin' hell in Cumberland Gap.

Daniel Boone on the Pinnacle Rock,
Daniel Boone on the Pinnacle Rock,
Daniel Boone on the Pinnacle Rock,
He killed Indians with an old flintlock.

Cumberland Gap is a noted place,
Cumberland Gap is a noted place,
Cumberland Gap is a noted place,
There's three kinds of water to wash your face.

Cumberland Gap with its cliffs and rocks,
Cumberland Gap with its cliffs and rocks,
Cumberland Gap with its cliffs and rocks,
The home of the panther, bear, and fox.

Me and my wife and our little chap,
Me and my wife and our little chap,
Me and my wife and our little chap,
All made a living in Cumberland Gap.

September morn in '62,
September morn in '62,
September morn in '62,
Morgan's Yankees all withdrew.

Oh, they spiked Long Tom on the mountain top.
Oh, they spiked Long Tom on the mountain top.
Oh, they spiked Long Tom on the mountain top.
And over the cliffs they let him drop.

They burned the hay, the meal, and meat,
They burned the hay, the meal, and meat,
They burned the hay, the meal, and meat,
And left the Rebels nothing to eat.

Braxton Bragg with his rebel band,
Braxton Bragg with his rebel band,
Braxton Bragg with his rebel band,
He ran George Morgan to the Bluegrass land.

Now Cumberland Gap is not very far,
Now Cumberland Gap is not very far,
Now Cumberland Gap is not very far,
It's just a little piece from Middlesbar.

◆ ◆ ◆

FRANCIS WARRINGTON DAWSON (1840—1889) was born in England. In 1862, came to the South on a blockade runner to volunteer for the Confederate Army. He served through the war and afterward became the able editor of the *Charleston News & Courier*.

Only a Private

Only a private! his jacket of gray

Is stained by the smoke and the dust;

As Bayard, he's brave; as Rupert, he's gay;

Reckless as Murat in heat of the fray,

But in God is his only trust!

Only a private! to march and to fight,

To suffer and starve and be strong;

With knowledge enough to know that the might

Of justice, and truth, and freedom and right,

In the end must crush out the wrong.

Only a private! no ribbon or star

Shall gild with false glory his name!

No honours for him in braid or in bar,

His Legion of Honour is only the scar,

And his wounds are his roll of fame!

Only a private! One more hero slain,
On the field lies silent and chill!
And in the far South a wife prays in vain
One clasp of the hand she may ne'er clasp again,
One kiss from the lips that are still.

Only a private! There let him sleep!
He will need nor tablet nor stone;
For the mosses and vines o'er his grave will creep,
And at night the stars through the clouds will peep,
And watch him who lies there alone.

Only a martyr! Who fought and who fell
Unknown and unmarked in the strife!
But still as he lies in his lonely cell,
Angel and Seraph the legend shall tell—
Such death is eternal life.

♦ ♦ ♦

"EATING GOOBER PEAS." The "goober peas" of this poem are, of course, peanuts. The pseudonymous publishers of the song stated that the lyrics were by A. Pindar, esq., pindar being another term for peanuts, and the lyrics by P. Nutt, esq.

Eating Goober Peas

Sitting by the roadside on a summer day,
Chatting with my mess-mates, passing time away,
Lying in the shadow underneath the tress,
Goodness, how delicious, eating goober peas!
Peas! peas! peas! peas! eating goober peas!
Goodness, how delicious, eating goober peas!

When a horseman passes the soldiers have a rule,
To cry out at their loudest, "Mister, here's your mule"; But
another pleasure, enchantinger than these,
Is wearing out your grinders, eating goober peas!
Just before the battle the Gen'ral hears a row.
He say, "The Yanks are coming, I hear their rifles now."
He turns around in wonder, and what do you think he sees?
The Georgia Militia, eating goober peas!

I think my song has lasted almost long enough;
The subject's interesting, but rhymes are mighty rough.
I wish this war was over, when free from rags and fleas,
We'd kiss our wives and sweethearts, and gobble goober peas!

♦ ♦ ♦

"ENLISTED TODAY"

Enlisted Today

I know the sun shines, and the lilacs are blowing,
And summer sends kisses by beautiful May—
Oh! to see all the treasures the spring is bestowing,
And think my boy Willie enlisted today,

It seems but a day since at twilight, low humming,
I rocked him to sleep with his cheek upon mine,
While Robby, the four-year old, watched for the coming
Of father, adown the street's indistinct line.

It is many a year since my Harry departed,
To come back no more in the twilight or dawn:
And Robby grew weary of watching, and started
Alone on the journey his father had gone.

It is many a year—and this afternoon sitting
At Robby's old window, I heard the band play,
And suddenly ceased dreaming over my knitting,
To recollect Willie is twenty today.

And that, standing beside him this soft May-day morning,
And the sun making gold of his wreathed cigar smoke,
I saw in his sweet eyes and lips a faint warning,
And choked down the tears when he eagerly spoke:

"Dear mother, you know how these Northmen are crowing,
They would trample the rights of the South in the dust,
The boys are all fire; and they wish I were going—"
He stopped, but his eyes said. "Oh, say if I must!"

I smiled on the boy, though my heart it seemed breaking,
My eyes filled with tears, so I turned them away,
And answered him, "Willie, 'tis well you are waking—
Go, act as your father would bid you, today!"

I sit in the window, and see the flags flying,
And drearily list to the roll of the drum,
And smother the pain in my heart that is lying
And bid all the fears in my bosom be dumb.

I shall sit in the window when summer is lying
Out over the fields, and the honey-bee's hum
Lulls the rose at the porch from her tremulous sighing,
And watch for the face of my darling to come.

And if he should fall-his young life he has given
For freedom's sweet sake; and for me, I will pray
Once more with my Harry and Robby in Heaven
To meet the dear boy who enlisted today.

◆ ◆ ◆

"FOR BALES." This effective Confederate satire of unknown authorship was apparently written in occupied New Orleans, to be sung to the music of the new and popular Yankee song "When Johnny Comes Marching Home." The satire concerns the Red River campaign in which a Union army and large fleet of gunboats and transports went upriver into northern Louisiana. They committed a great deal of destruction and theft in an area of the South not yet invaded but were defeated by a small Confederate force under General Richard Taylor. The "ring" refers to a plot of Lincolnian money men to get rich with confiscated cotton. The defeat chastened the Presidential ambitions of the Massachusetts General Banks, but made him, Admiral Porter, and other Northerners rich men. The steamboat disaster of the Sultana, in which 1,800 Union soldiers perished, was due to the diversion of shipping to cotton stealing.

For Bales

We all went down to New Orleans,

For Bales, for Bales;

We all went down to New Orleans,

For Bales, says I;

We all went down to New Orleans,

To get a peep behind the scenes,

"And we'll all drink stone blind,

Johnny fill up the bowl."

We thought when we go in the "Ring,"

For Bales, for Bales;

We thought when we got in the "Ring,"

For Bales, says I;

We thought when we got in the "Ring,"
Greenbacks would be a dead sure thing,
"And we'll all drink stone blind,
Johnny fill up the bowl."

The "ring" went up, with bagging and rope,
For Bales, for Bales;
Upon the "Black Hawk" with bagging and rope,
For Bales, says I;
Went up "Red River" with bagging and rope,
Expecting to make a pile of "soap,"
"And we'll all drink stone blind,
Johnny fill up the bowl."

But Taylor and Smith, with ragged ranks,
For Bales, for Bales;
But Taylor and Smith, with ragged ranks,
For Bales, says I;
But Taylor and Smith, with ragged ranks,
Burned up the cotton and whipped old Banks,
"And we'll all drink stone blind,
Johnny fill up the bowl."

Our "ring" came back and cursed and swore,
For Bales, for Bales;
Our "ring" came back and cursed and swore,
For Bales, says I;
Our "ring" came back and cursed and swore,
For we got no cotton at Grand Ecore,
"And we'll all drink stone blind,
Johnny fill up the bowl."

Now let us all give praise and thanks,
For Bales, for Bales;
Now let us all give praise and thanks,
For Bales, says I;
Now let us all give praise and thanks,
For the victory gained by General Banks,
"And we'll all drink stone blind,
Johnny fill up the bowl."

♦ ♦ ♦

"JINE THE CALVARY" This rollicking song appeared in 1862, to be sung to the tune of "Home Alabama." One cannot hear the tune without thinking of Sweeney, the great banjo artist who rode with J.E.B. Stuart.

Jine the Calvary

If you want to have a good time,
    jine the cavalry!
Jine the cavalry! Jine the cavalry!
If you want to catch the Devil,
    if you want to have fun,
If you want to smell Hell, jine the cavalry!

We're the boys who went around McClellian,
Went around McClellian, went around McClellian!
We're the boys who went around McClellian,
Bully boys, hey! Bully boys, ho!

If you want to have a good time,
    jine the cavalry!
Jine the cavalry! Jine the cavalry!
If you want to catch the Devil,
    if you want to have fun,
If you want to smell Hell, jine the cavalry!

We're the boys who crossed the Potomicum,
Crossed the Potomicum, crossed the Potomicum!
We're the boys who crossed the Potomicum,
Bully boys, hey! Bully boys, ho!

If you want to have a good time,
    jine the cavalry!
Jine the cavalry! Jine the cavalry!
If you want to catch the Devil,
    if you want to have fun,
If you want to smell Hell, jine the cavalry!

Then we went into Pennsylvania,
Into Pennsylvania, into Pennsylvania!
Then we went into Pennsylvania,
Bully boys, hey! Bully boys, ho!

If you want to have a good time,
    jine the cavalry!
Jine the cavalry! Jine the cavalry!
If you want to catch the Devil,
    if you want to have fun,
If you want to smell Hell, jine the cavalry!

The big fat Dutch gals hand around
    the breadium,
Hand around the breadium,
    hand around the breadium!
The big fat Dutch gals hand around
    the breadium,
Bully boys, hey! Bully boys, ho!

If you want to have a good time,
        jine the cavalry!
Jine the cavalry! Jine the cavalry!
If you want to catch the Devil,
        if you want to have fun,
If you want to smell Hell, jine the cavalry!

Ol Joe Hooker, won't you come out of
        The Wilderness?
Come out of The Wilderness,
        come out of The Wilderness?
Ol' Joe Hooker, won't you come out of
        The Wilderness?
Bully boys, hey! Bully boys, ho!

If you want to have a good time,
        jine the cavalry!
Jine the cavalry! Jine the cavalry!
If you want to catch the Devil,
        if you want to have fun,
If you want to smell Hell, jine the cavalry!

◆ ◆ ◆

MARIE RAVENEL DE LA COSTE. Not much is known about this lady except that she was born in 1839, probably in Savannah, to French immigrant parents. This, her only known work, obviously reflects nursing in Savannah Confederate hospitals. "Somebody's Darling," put to music was extremely popular on both sides during the war.

Somebody's Darling

Into a ward of the whitewashed halls,
Where the dead and the dying lay—
Wounded by bayonets, shells and balls,
Somebody's darling was borne one day
Somebody's darling, so young and so brave!
Wearing yet on his sweet, pale face
Soon to be hid in the dust of the grave—
The lingering light of his boyhood's grace!

Matted and damp are the curls of gold
Kissing the snow of that fair young brow,
Pale are the lips of delicate mould,
Somebody's darling is dying now.
Back from his beautiful blue-veined brow
Brush his wandering waves of gold;
Cross his hands on his bosom now—
Somebody's darling is still and cold.

Kiss him once for somebody's sake,
Murmur a prayer soft and low—
One bright curl from its fair mates take
They were somebody's pride you know,
Somebody's hand hath rested there;
Was it a mother's, soft and white?
Or have the lips of a sister fair
Been baptized in their waves of light?

God knows best! He has somebody's love;
Somebody's heart enshrined him there,
Somebody wafted his name above,
Night and morn, on the wings of prayer.
Somebody wept when he marched away,
Looking so handsome, brave and grand!
Somebody's kiss on his forehead lay
Somebody clung to his parting hand.

Somebody's watching and waiting for him,
Yearning to hold him again to her heart;
And there he lies with his blue eyes dim,
And the smiling, child-like lips apart.
Tenderly bury the fair young dead—
Pausing to drop on his grave a tear;
Carve on the wooden slab o'er his head:
"Somebody's darling slumbers here."

◆ ◆ ◆

WILLIAM GORDON McCABE (1841—1920) left the University of Virginia to join the elite Confederate Richmond Howitzers, serving throughout the war. He was afterwards, a distinguished author, poet, translator, textbook author, and president of the Virginia Historical Society.

Christmas Night of '62

The wintry blast goes wailing by,
    The snow is falling overhead;
    I hear the lonely sentry's tread,
And distant watch-fires light the sky.

Dim forms go flitting through the gloom;
    The soldiers cluster round the blaze
    To talk of other Christmas days,
And softly speak of home and home.

My sabre swinging overhead
    Gleams in the watch-fire's fitful glow,
    While fiercely drives the blinding snow,
And memory leads me to the dead.

My thoughts go wandering to and fro,
    Vibrating between the Now and Then;
    I see the low-browed home again,
The old hall wreathed with mistletoe.

And sweetly from the far-off years
    Comes borne the laughter faint and low,
    The voices of the Long Ago!
My eyes are wet with tender tears.

I feel again the mother-kiss,
    I see again the glad surprise
    That lightened up the tranquil eyes
And brimmed them o'er with tears of bliss,

As, rushing from the old hall-door,
    She fondly clasped her wayward boy—
    Her face all radiant with the joy
She felt to see him home once more.

My sabre swinging on the bough
    Gleams in the watch-fire's fitful glow,
    While fiercely drives the blinding snow
Aslant upon my saddened brow.

Those cherished faces all
    Asleep within the quiet graves
    Where lies the snow in drifting waves, —
And I am sitting here alone.

There's not a comrade here to-night
    But knows that loved ones far away
    On bended knee this night will pray:
"God bring our darling from the fight."

But there are none to wish me back,
    For me no yearning prayers arise.
    The lips are mute and closed the eyes—
My home is in the bivouac.

♦ ♦ ♦

JOHN C. McLEMORE (d. 1862). This poet is identified, uncertainly, as one who was killed early in the war at the battle of Seven Pines. Francis Bartow and Felix Zollicoffer were Confederate generals killed early in the war.

The Rappahannock Army Song

The toil of the march is over—
The pack will be borne no more—
For we've come for the help of Richmond,
From the Rappahannock's shore.
The foe is closing round us—
We can hear his ravening cry;
So, ho! for fair old Richmond!
Like soldiers we'll do or die.

We have left the land that bore us,
Full many a league away,
And our mothers and sisters miss us,
As with tearful eyes they pray;
But this will repress their weeping,
And still the rising sigh—
For all, for fair old Richmond,
Have come to do or die.

We have come to join our brothers
    From the proud Dominion's vales,
And to meet the dark-cheeked soldier,
    Tanned by the Tropic gales;
To greet them all full gladly,
    With hand and beaming eye,
And to swear for fair old Richmond,
    We all will do or die.

The fair Carolina sisters
    Stand ready, lance in hand,
To fight as they did in an older war,
    For the sake of their fatherland.
The glories of Sumter and Bethel
    Have raised their fame full high,
But they'll fade, if for fair old Richmond
    They swear not to do or die,

Zollicoffer looks down on his people,
    And trusts to their hearts and arms,
To avenge the blood he has shed,
    In the midst of the battle's alarms.
Alabamians, remember the past,
    Be the " South at Manassas," their cry;
As onward for fair old Richmond,
    They marched to do or die.

Brave Bartow, from home on high,
    Calls the Empire State to the front,
To bear once more as she has borne
    With glory the battle's brunt.
Mississippians who know no surrender,
    Bear the flag of the Chief on high;
For he, too, for fair old Richmond,
    Has sworn to do or die.

Fair land of my birth—sweet Florida—
    Your arm is weak, but your soul
Must tell of a purer, holier strength,
    When the drums for the battle roll.
Look within, for your hope in the combat,
    Nor think of your few with a sigh—
If you win not for fair old Richmond,
    At least you can bravely die.

Onward all! Oh! Band of brothers!
    The beat of the long roll's heard!
And the hearts of the columns advancing
    By the sound of its music stirred.
Onward all! And never return,
    Till our foes from the borders fly—
To be crowned by the fair of old Richmond,
    As those who could do or die.

◆ ◆ ◆

"MOTHER LINCOLN'S MELODIES"

Mother Lincoln's Melodies

Little Be-Pope,
He lost his hope,
"Coz" Jackson he couldn't find him.
He found him at last,
And ran very fast,
With his tail hanging down behind him.

Poor Johnnie Pope
Has lost his coat,
But let him never mind it;
When he comes down
To Richmond town,
There he'll be sure to find it.

Pope and McDowell
Fighting for a town,
Up jumped General Lee
And knocked 'em both down.

Burnside, Burnside,
whither doth thou wander?
Up stream, down stream,
like a crazy gander?

The man in the North,
He pledged his troth,
To find a Richmond barber,
But the man in the South,
He mashed his mouth
At a place they call Cold Harbor.

Old Mother Seward,
She went to the Lee-ward,
To get her dog a Union bone.
She got to Manassas,
And saw them harass us—
Lord! How Mother Seward did groan.

Yankee was a bad man,
Yankee was a thief,
Yankee came to my house
and stole a side of beef;
I went to Yankee's house,
Yankee he had fled,
Caught him on the battle-field,
and there I killed him dead.

♦ ♦ ♦

JOHN LOUIS O'SULLIVAN (1813—1895). O'Sullivan is an example of a Northern patriotic American who sought exile when the War for Southern Independence broke out and vigorously used his pen to support the Confederacy in Europe. He came from a family of Irish émigrés and soldiers of fortune. During the antebellum period he was a national leader of the Democratic party as editor of the *Democratic Review* in New York. He coined the famous phrase "manifest destiny" and was appointed by President Pierce as U.S. Minister to Portugal. He participated in efforts to liberate Cuba and strongly opposed Lincoln's coercion of the South.

Close The Ranks

THE fell invader is before!
Close the ranks! Close up the ranks!
We'll hunt his legions from our shore,
Close the ranks! Close up the ranks!
Our wives, our children are behind,
Our mothers, sisters, dear and kind,
Their voices reach us on the wind,
Close the ranks! Close up the ranks!

Are we to bend to slavish yoke?
Close the ranks! Close up the ranks!
We'll bend when bends our Southern oak.
Close the ranks! Close up the ranks!
On with the line of serried steel,
We all can die, we none can kneel
To crouch beneath the Northern heel.
Close the ranks! Close up the ranks!

We kneel to God, and God alone.
Close the ranks! Close up the ranks!
One heart in all—all hearts as one.
Close the ranks! Close up the ranks!
For home, for country, truth and right,
We stand or fall in freedom's fight:
In such a cause the right is might.
Close the ranks! Close up the ranks!

We're here from every Southern home.
Close the ranks! Close up the ranks!
Fond, weeping voices bade us come.
Close the ranks! Close up the ranks!
The husband, brother, boy, and sire,
All burning with one holy fire
Our country's love our only hire.
Close the ranks! Close up the ranks!

We cannot fail, we will not yield!
Close the ranks! Close up the ranks!
Our bosoms are our country's shield.
Close the ranks! Close up the ranks!
By Washington's immortal name,
By Stonewall Jackson's kindred fame,
Their souls, their deeds, their cause the same,
Close the ranks! Close up the ranks!

By all we hope, by all we love,
Close the ranks! Close up the ranks!
By home on earth, by Heaven above,
Close the ranks! Close up the ranks!
By all the tears, and heart's blood shed,
By all our hosts of martyred dead,
We'll conquer, or we'll share their bed.
Close the ranks! Close up the ranks!

The front may fall, the rear succeed,
Close the ranks! Close up the ranks!
We smile in triumph as we bleed,
Close the ranks! Close up the ranks!
Our Southern Cross above us waves,
Long shall it bless the sacred graves
Of those who died, but were not slaves.
Close the ranks! Close up the ranks!

♦ ♦ ♦

JOHN WILLIAMSON PALMER (1825—1906) of Maryland is generally considered the author of these lyrics. He claimed to be the first physician in San Francisco and to have served as a physician with the British East Company during war in Burma. During the War to Prevent Southern Independence he was a "roving correspondent" for the *New York Tribune*. As far as can be determined "Stonewall Jackson's Way" was first published in 1862 in New York, said to have been found on the body of a Confederate soldier because Palmer feared arrest.

Stonewall Jackson's Way

Come, stack arms, men! pile on the rails,
    Stir up the camp-fire bright;
No growling if the canteen fails,
    We'll make a roaring night.
Here Shenandoah brawls along,
There burly Blue Ridge echoes strong,
To swell the Brigade's rousing song
    Of "Stonewall Jackson's way."

We see him now—the queer slouched hat
    Cocked o'er his eye askew;
The shrewd, dry smile; the speech so pat,
    So calm, so blunt, so true.
The "Blue-light Elder" knows 'em well;
Says he, "That's Banks—he's fond of shell;
Lord save his soul! we'll give him—" well!
    That's "Stonewall Jackson's way."

Silence! Ground arms! Kneel all! Caps off!
  Old Massa's goin' to pray.
Strangle the fool that dares to scoff!
  Attention! It's his way.
Appealing from his native sod
In *forma pauperis* to God:
"Lay bare Thine arm; stretch forth Thy rod!
  Amen!" That's Stonewall's way."

He's in the saddle now. Fall in!
  Steady! the whole brigade!
Hill's at the ford, cut off; we'll win
  His way out, ball and blade!
What matter if our shoes are worn?
What matter if our feet are torn?
"Quick step! we're with him before morn!"
  That's "Stonewall Jackson's way."

The sun's bright lances rout the mists
    Of morning, and, by George!
Here's Longstreet, struggling in the lists,
    Hemmed in an ugly gorge.
Pope and his Dutchmen, whipped before;
"Bay'nets and grape!" hear Stonewall roar;
"Charge, Stuart! Pay off Ashby's score!"
    In "Stonewall Jackson's way."

Ah, Maiden! wait and watch and yearn
    For news of Stonewall's band.
Ah, Widow! read, with eyes that burn,
    That ring upon thy hand.
Ah, Wife! sew on, pray on, hope on;
Thy life shall not be all forlorn;
The foe had better ne'er been born
    That gets in "Stonewall's way."

♦ ♦ ♦

WILLIAM DENNISON PORTER (1810—1883) of South
Carolina was a Charleston lawyer and president of the State
Senate.

45

My Country

Go, READ the stories of the great and free,
The nations on the long, bright roll of fame,
Whose noble rage has baffled the decree
Of tyrants to despoil their life and name;

Whose swords have flashed like lightning in the eyes
Of robber despots, glorying in their might,
And taught the world, by deeds of high emprise,
The power of truth and sacredness of right:

Whose people, strong to suffer and endure,
In faith have wrestled till the blessing came,
And won through woes a victory doubly sure,
As martyr wins his crown through blood and flame,

46

The purest virtue has been sorest tried,
Nor is there glory without patient toil;
And he who woes fair Freedom for his bride,
Through suffering must be purged of stain and soil.

My country! In this hour of trial sore,
When in the balance trembling hangs thy fate,
Brace thy great heart with courage to the core,
Not let one jot of faith or hope abate!

The world's bright eye is fixed upon thee still;
Life, honour, fame these all are in the scale;
Endure! Endure! Endure! With iron will,
And by the truth of heaven, thou shalt not fail.

◆ ◆ ◆

"REBELS"

Rebels

Rebels! 'tis a holy name!
　　The name our fathers bore,
When battling in the cause of Right,
　　Against the tyrant in his might,
In the dark days of yore.

Rebels! 'tis our family name!
Our father, Washington,
Was the arch-rebel in the fight,
And gave the name to use,—a right
Of father unto son.

Rebels! 'tis our given name!
　　Our mother, Liberty,
Received the title with her fame,
In days of grief, of fear, and shame,
　　When at her breast were we.

Rebels! 'tis our sealed name!
　　A baptism of blood!
The war—aye, and the din of strife—
The fearful contest, life for life—
　　The mingled crimson flood.

Rebels! 'tis a patriot's name!
    In struggles it was given;
We bore it then when tyrants raved
And through their curses 'twas engraved
    On the doomsday-book of heaven.

Rebels! 'tis our fighting name!
    For peace rules o'er the land,
Until they speak of craven woe—
Until our rights receive a blow,
    From foe's or brother's hand.

Rebels! 'tis our dying name!
    For, although life is dear,
Yet, freemen born and freemen bred,
We'd rather live as freemen dead,
    Than live in slavish fear.

Then call us rebels if you will—
    We glory in the name;
For bending under unjust laws,
And swearing faith to an unjust cause,
    We count a greater shame.

◆ ◆ ◆

"THE RETURN"

The Return

THREE years! I wonder if she'll know me?
I limp a little, and I left one arm
At Petersburg; and I am grown as brown
As the plump chestnuts on my little farm:
And I'm as shaggy as the chestnut burrs—
But ripe and sweet within, and wholly hers.

The darling! How I long to see her!
My heart outruns this feeble soldier pace,
For I remember, after I had left,
A little Charlie came to take my place,
Ah! How the laughing, three-year-old, brown eyes
His mother's eyes will stare with pleased surprise!

Surely, they will be at the corner watching!
I sent them word that I should come to-night:
The birds all know it, for they crowd around,
Twittering their welcome with a wild delight;
And that old robin, with a halting wing —
I saved her life, three years ago last spring.

Three years! Perhaps I am but dreaming!
For, like the pilgrim of the long ago,
I've tugged, a weary burden at my back,
Through summer's heat and winter's blinding snow;
Till now, I reach my home, my darling's breast,
There I can roll my burden off, and rest.

When morning came, the early rising sun
Laid his light fingers on a soldier sleeping—
Where a soft covering of bright green grass
Over two mounds was lightly creeping;
But waked him not: his was the rest eternal,
Where the brown eyes reflected love supernal.

◆ ◆ ◆

"ROLL, ALABAMA, ROLL." The authorship of this song, still widely played, is unknown but is variously suggested. It is sometimes cited as "an English folk song." It does resemble an English sea shanty. Another suggestion to the origin is that it was put together by a member of the crew of the *CSS Alabama*, Frank Townsend. The best conjecture is perhaps that it began as a South African folk song arising from the *Alabama's* visit to Cape Town.

Roll, Alabama, Roll

When the Alabama's keel was laid
  Roll, Alabama, roll!
It was laid in the yard of Jonathan Laird
  Oh, roll, Alabama, roll!

It was laid in the yard of Jonathan Laird
It was laid in the town of Birkenhead

Across the Mersey river she sailed then
And Liverpool fitted her with guns and men

From the Western Isles she sailed forth
To destroy all commerce of the North

Down to Cherbourg came she straight one day
For to take her toll in prize money

There many a sailor lad met his doom
When the ship Kearsarge hove in view

And a shot from the forward pivot that day
It shot the Alabama's stern away

In the three-mile limit, in sixty-five
The Alabama sunk to her grave

◆ ◆ ◆

"A SOLDIER'S WIFE"

Victories of the Heart

There's not a stately hall,
There's not a cottage fair,
That proudly stands on Southern soil,
Or softly nestles there,
But in its peaceful walls
With wealth or comfort blessed,
A stormy battle fierce hath raged
In gentle woman's breast.

There Love, the true, the brave,
The beautiful, the strong,
Wrestles with Duty, gaunt and stern, —
Wrestles and struggles long.
He falls, no more again
His giant foe to meet;
Bleeding at every opening vein,
Love falls at Duty's feet.

'O Daughter of the South!
No victor's crown be thine,
Not thine upon the tented field
In martial pomp to shine;

But with unfaltering trust
In Him who rules on high,
To deck thy loved ones for the fray,
And send them forth to die.

She, the tried, the true,
The loving wife of years,
Chokes down the rising agony,
Drives back the starting tears;
"I yield thee up," she cries,
"In the country's cause to fight;
Strike for our own, our children's home,
And God defend the right."

O Daughter of the South!
When our fair land is free,
When peace her lovely mantle throws
Softly o'er land and sea,
History shall tell how thou
Hast nobly borne thy part,
And won the proudest triumph yet—
The victory of the heart.

◆ ◆ ◆

"SONG OF THE TEXAS RANGERS"

Song of the Texas Rangers

The morning star is paling,
The camp-fires flicker low;
Our steeds are madly neighing,
For the bugle bids us go.
So put the foot in stirrup,
And shake the bridle free,
For to-day the Texas Rangers
Must cross the Tennessee.
With Wharton for our leader,
We'll chase the dastard foe,
Till our horses bathe their fetlocks
In the deep blue Ohio.

Our men are from the prairies,
That roll broad and proud and free,
From the high and craggy mountains
To the murmuring Mexic sea;
And their hearts are open as their plains,
Their thoughts are proudly brave
As the bold cliffs of the San Bernard,
Or the Gulfs resistless wave.
Then quick into the saddle,
And shake the bridle free,
Today with gallant Wharton,
We cross the Tennessee.

'Tis joy to be a Ranger!
To fight for dear Southland;
'Tis joy to follow Wharton,
With his gallant, trusty band!
'Tis joy to see our Harrison,
Plunge, like a meteor bright
Into the thickest of the fray,
And deal his deathly might.
Oh! who'd not be a Ranger,
And follow Wharton's cry!
To battle for his country—
And, if it needs be-die!

By the Colorado's waters,
On the Gulf's deep murmuring shore,
On our soft green peaceful prairies
Are the homes we may see no more;
But in those homes our gentle wives,
And mothers with silv'ry hairs,
Are loving us with tender hearts,
And shielding us with prayers.
So, trusting in our country's God,
We draw our stout, good brand,
For those we love at home,
Our altars and our land.

Up, up with the crimson battle-flag!
Let the blue pennon fly;
Our steeds are stamping proudly—
They hear the battle-cry!
The thundering bomb, the bugle's call,
Proclaim the foe is near;
We strike for God and native land,
And all we hold most dear.
Then spring into the saddle,
And shake the bridle free,
For Wharton leads, through fire and blood,
For home and Victory!

♦ ♦ ♦

"THE TEXAN MARSEILLAISE"

The Texan Marseillaise

Sons of the South, arouse to battle!
Gird on your armor for the fight!
The Northern Thugs with dread "War's rattle,"
Pour on each vale, and glen, and height;
Meet them as Ocean meets in madness
The frail bark on the rocky shore,
When crested billows foam and roar,
And the wrecked crew go down in sadness.

CHORUS —
Arm! Arm! Ye Southern braves!
Scatter yon Vandal hordes!
Despots and bandits, fitting food
For vultures and your swords.

Shall dastard tyrants march their legions
To crush the land of Jackson-Lee?
Shall freedom fly to other regions,
And sons of Yorktown bend the knee?
Or shall their "footprints' base pollution"
Of Southern soil, in blood be purged,
And every flying slave be scourged
Back to his snows in wild confusion?

CHORUS —

Vile despots, with their minions knavish,
Would drag us back to their embrace;
Will freemen brook a chain so slavish?
Will brave men take so low a place?
O, Heaven! for words-the loathing, scorning
We feel for such a Union's bands:
To paint with more than mortal hands,
And sound our loudest notes of warning.

CHORUS —

What! Union with a race ignoring
The charter of our nation's birth!
Union with bastard slaves adoring
The fiend that chains them to the earth!
No! we reply in tones of thunder—
No! our staunch hills fling back the sound—
No! our hoarse cannon echo round
No! evermore remain asunder!

CHORUS —

Arm! Arm! Ye Southern braves!
Scatter yon Vandal hordes!
Despots and bandits, fitting food
For vultures and your swords.

♦ ♦ ♦

SEVERN TEACKLE WALLIS (1816—1894) of Maryland was an occasional author during a busy legal and political career for the Democratic party and against the Republicans, before, during, and after the War.

The Guerrillas: A Southern War-Song

"Awake! and to horse, my brothers!
For the dawn is glimmering gray;
And hark! in the crackling brushwood
There are feet that tread this way.

"Who cometh?" "A friend." "What tidings?"
"O God! I sicken to tell,
For the earth seems earth no longer,
And its sights are sights of hell!

"There's rapine and fire and slaughter,
From the mountain down to the shore;
There's blood on the trampled harvest—
There's blood on the homestead floor.

"From the far-off conquered cities
Comes the voice of a stifled wail;
And the shrieks and moans of the houseless
Ring out, like a dirge, on the gale.

"I've seen, from the smoking village,
Our mothers and daughters fly;
I've seen where the little children
Sank down, in the furrows, to die.

"On the banks of the battle-stained river
I stood, as the moonlight shone,
And it glared on the face of my brother,
As the sad wave swept him on.

"Where my home was glad, are ashes,
And horror and shame had been there—
For I found, on the fallen lintel,
This tress of my wife's torn hair.

"They are turning the slave upon us,
And, with more than the fiend's worst art,
Have uncovered the fires of the savage
That slept in his untaught heart.

"The ties to our hearths that bound him,
They have rent, with curses, away,
And maddened him, with their madness,
To be almost as brutal as they.

"With halter and torch and Bible,
And hymns to the sound of the drum,
They preach the gospel of Murder,
And pray for Lust's kingdom to come.

"To saddle! to saddle! my brothers!
Look up to the rising sun,
And ask of the God who shines there,
Whether deeds like these shall be done!

"In God's hand, alone, is judgment;
But He strikes with the hands of men,
And His blight would wither our manhood
If we smote not the smiter again.

"By the graves where our fathers slumber,
By the shrines where our mothers prayed,
By our homes and hopes and freedom,
Let every man swear on his blade,—

"That he will not sheath nor stay it,
Till from point to heft it glow
With the flush of Almighty vengeance,
In the blood of the felon foe.

"Wherever the vandal cometh,
Press home to his heart with your steel,
And when at his bosom you cannot,
Like the serpent, go strike at his heel!

"Through thicket and wood go hunt him,
Creep up to his camp fireside,
And let ten of his corpses blacken
Where one of our brothers hath died.

"In his fainting, foot-sore marches,
In his flight from the stricken fray,
In the snare of the lonely ambush,
The debts that we owe him pay.

They swore and the answering sunlight
Leapt red from their lifted swords,
And the hate in their hearts made echo
To the wrath in their burning words.

There's weeping in all New England,
And by Schuylkill's banks a knell,
And the widows there, and the orphans,
How the oath was kept can tell.

♦ ♦ ♦

"THE YELLOW ROSE OF TEXAS." This song was popular with Confederate soldiers. A new last verse was added after Hood's disastrous Tennessee campaign.

The Yellow Rose of Texas

There's a yellow rose in Texas,
    that I am going to see,
No other darky knows her,
    no darky only me
She cryed so when I left her
    it like to broke my heart,
And if I ever find her,
    we nevermore will part.

CHORUS —
She's the sweetest rose of color
    this darky ever knew,
Her eyes are bright as diamonds,
    they sparkle like the dew;
You may talk about your Dearest May,
    and sing of Rosa Lee,
But the Yellow Rose of Texas
    beats the belles of Tennessee.

When The Rio Grande is flowing,
    the starry skies are bright,
She walks along the river
    in the quiet summer night:
She thinks if I remember,
    when we parted long ago,
I promised to come back again,
    and not to leave her so.

CHORUS —
She's the sweetest rose of color
    this darky ever knew,
Her eyes are bright as diamonds,
    they sparkle like the dew;
You may talk about your Dearest May,
    and sing of Rosa Lee,
But the Yellow Rose of Texas
    beats the belles of Tennessee.

Oh now I'm going to find her,
    for my heart is full of woe,
And we'll sing the songs together,
    that we sung so long ago
We'll play the bango gaily,
    and we'll sing the songs of yore,
And the Yellow Rose of Texas
    shall be mine forevermore.

CHORUS —
She's the sweetest rose of color
    this darky ever knew,
Her eyes are bright as diamonds,
    they sparkle like the dew;
You may talk about your Dearest May,
    and sing of Rosa Lee,
But the Yellow Rose of Texas
    beats the belles of Tennessee.

(New verse by Confederate soldiers after Hood's Tennessee campaign)

Oh my feet are torn and bloody,
    and my heart is full of woe,
I'm going back to Georgia,
    to find my Uncle Joe,
You may talk about your Beauregard,
    and sing of Bobby Lee,
But the gallant Hood of Texas,
    played hell in Tennessee.

♦ ♦ ♦

II. Facing Defeat

How could we help falling on our knees, all of us together, and praying God to pity and forgive us all.

—Gen. Joshua Chamberlain,

U.S. Army, at Appomattox

ROBERT EDWARD LEE (1807—1870) of Virginia was, of course, one of history's great soldiers and the commander of one of history's great armies. Not well-known, because he never made a show of it, is that Lee was a man of g learning, insight, and eloquence. His last order to his army at Appomattox (below), one of the most moving documents in American history, approaches the poetic. His postbellum comments to trusted correspondents provide the best brief historical summary of the cause and result of the War for Southern Independence.

Farewell to the Army of Northern Virginia

Headquarters, Army of Northern Virginia,
11 April 1865

General Order No. 9

After four years of arduous service, marked by unsurpassed courage and fortitude, the Army of Northern Virginia has been compelled to yield to overwhelming numbers and resources.

I need not tell the survivors of so many hard fought battles who have remained steadfast to the last, that I have consented to this result from no distrust of them.

But feeling that valour and devotion could accomplish nothing that could compensate for the loss that would have attended the continuance of the contest, I determined to avoid the useless sacrifice of those whose past services have endeared them to their country.

By the terms of the agreement, officers and men can return to their homes and remain until exchanged. You will take with you the satisfaction that proceeds from the consciousness of duty faithfully performed, and I earnestly pray that a merciful God will extend to you his blessing and protection.

With an unceasing admiration of your constancy and devotion to your country and a grateful remembrance of your kind and generous consideration for myself I bid you an affectionate farewell.

♦

Postbellum Comments

Letter to Chauncey Burr, New York
Jan. 5 1866

....All that the South has ever desired was that the Union, as established by our forefathers, should be preserved, and that the government as originally organised should be administered in purity and truth....

We could have pursued no other course without dishonour. And sad as the results have been, if it had all to be done over again, we should be compelled to act in precisely the same manner.

♦

Letter to Lord Acton

15 Dec. 1866

....while I have considered the preservation of the constitutional power of the General Government to be the foundation of our peace and safety at home and abroad, I yet believe that the maintenance of the rights and authority reserved to the states and to the people, not only essential to the adjustment and balance of the general system, but the safeguard to the continuance of a free government. I consider it as the chief source of stability to our political system, whereas the consolidation of the states into one vast republic, sure to be aggressive abroad and despotic at home, will be the certain precursor of that ruin which has overwhelmed all that have preceded it....

◆ ◆ ◆

MARGARET JUNKIN PRESTON (1820—1897) of Lexington, Virginia, was the sister of Stonewall Jackson's first wife who died tragically young. Mrs. Preston wrote stirring patriotic poetry during The War. The first poem was written in response to the defeat of the Confederacy. The second concerns the brutal imprisonment of President Davis. Regulus was a Roman hero who never yielded under torture by the Carthaginian barbarians. The third was written on the death of General Lee In 1870.

Acceptation

We do accept thee, heavenly Peace!

Albeit thou comest in a guise

Unlooked for—undesired, our eyes

Welcome through tears the sweet release

From war, and woe, and want,—surcease,

For which we bless thee, blessed Peace!

We lift our foreheads from the dust;

And as we meet thy brow's clear calm,

There falls a freshening sense of balm

Upon our spirits. Fear—distrust—

The hopeless present on us thrust—

We'll meet them as we can, and must.

War has not wholly wrecked us: still
Strong hands, brave hearts, high souls are ours—
Proud consciousness of quenchless powers—
A Past whose memory makes us thrill—
Futures uncharactered, to fill
With heroisms—if we will.

Then courage, brothers!—Though each breast
Feel oft the rankling thorn, despair,
That failure plants so sharply there
No pain, no pang shall be confest:
We'll work and watch the brightening west,
And leave to God and Heaven the rest.

♦

Regulus

I.

HAVE ye no mercy? Punic rage
Boasted small skill in torture, when
The sternest patriot of his age
And Romans all were patriots then—
Was doomed, with his unwinking eyes,
To stand beneath the fiery skies,
Until the sun-shafts pierced his brain,
And he grew blind with poignant pain,
While Carthage jeered and taunted. Yet,
When day's slow-moving orb had set,
And pitying Nature — kind to all —
In dewy darkness bathed her hand,
And laid it on each lidless ball,
So crazed with gusts of scorching sand, —
They yielded, nor forbade the grace
By flashing torches in his face.

II.

Ye flash the torches! Never night
Brings the blank dark to that worn eye:
In pitiless, perpetual light,
Our tortured Regulus must lie!
Yet tropic suns seemed tender; they
Eyed not with purpose to betray:
No human vengeance, like a spear
Whetted to sharpness, keen and clear,
By settled hatred, pricked its way
Right through the blood-shot iris!—Nay,
Ye are refined torment. Glare
A little longer through the bars,
At the bay'd lion in his lair,—
And God's dear hand, from out the stars,
To shame inhuman man, may cast
Its shadow o'er those lids at last,
And end their aching, with the blest
Signet and seal of perfect rest!

♦

Gone Forward

Yes, "Let the tent be struck." Victorious morning
Through every crevice flashes in a day
Magnificent beyond all earth's adorning:
The night is over; wherefore should he stay?
And wherefore should our voices choke to say,
"The General has gone forward"?

Life's foughten field not once beheld surrender;
But with superb endurance, present, past,
Our pure Commander, lofty, simple, tender,
Through good, through ill, held his high purpose fast,
Wearing his armor spotless—till at last,
Death gave the final, "Forward."

All hearts grew sudden palsied: Yet what said he
Thus summoned?—"Let the tent be struck!"—For when
Did call of duty fail to find him ready
Nobly to do his work in sight of men,
For God's and for his country's sake and then
To watch, wait, or go forward?

We will not weep—we dare not! Such a story
As his large life writes on the century's years,
Should crowd our bosoms with a flush of glory,
That manhood's type, supremest that appears
To-day, he shows the ages. Nay, no tears
Because he has gone forward!

Gone forward? —Whither? —Where the marshall'd legions,
Christ's well-worn soldiers, from their conflicts cease;—
Where Faith's true Red-Cross knights repose in regions
Thick-studded with the calm, white tents of peace—
Thither, right joyful to accept release,
The General has gone forward!

♦ ♦ ♦

JAMES INNES RANDOLPH (1837–1887) of Virginia did not take defeat lightly. A lawyer, engineer, newspaper editor, and talented amateur actor and musician, he served as a captain on Gen. J.E.B. Stuart's staff. Set to music with the Irish air "Joe Brewer," "Oh, I'm a Good Old Rebel," is still sung with gusto. The song collector Frank Dobie found the song being sung by cowboys in the early 20th century and thought it was of folk origin. In postbellum years, Randolph was a prominent journalist in Baltimore and continued to be a serious poet. He appears again in Vol. 4 of *Southern Poets and Poems*.

Oh, I'm a Good Old Rebel

Oh, I'm a good old Rebel,

Now that's just what I am;

For this "fair land of Freedom"

I do not care a damn.

I'm glad I fit against it—

I only wish we'd won.

And I don't want no pardon

For anything I've done.

I hates the Constitution,

This great Republic too;

I hates the Freedmen's Buro,

In uniforms of blue.

I hates the nasty eagle,

With all his brag and fuss;

But the lyin', thievin' Yankees

I hates' em wuss and wuss.

I hates the Yankee nation
And everything they do,
I hates the Declaration
of Independence, too;
I hates the glorious Union
Tis drippin' with our blood
I hates their striped banner,
I fit it all I could.

I followed Ol' Marse Robert
for four years, nearabout,
got wounded in three places
and starved at P'int Lookout:
I cotched the rheumatism
a'campin' in the snow;
but I killed a chance o' Yankees,
I'd like to kill some mo'.

We got three hundred thousand
Befo' they conquered us.
They died of Southern fever
And Southern steel and shot;
And I wish it was three million
Instead of what we got.

I can't take up my musket
And fight' em now no mo',
But I ain't a-goin' to love' em,
Now that is sartin sho';
And I don't want no pardon
For what I was and am;
And I won't be reconstructed,
And I do not give a damn.

♦

Twilight at Hollywood

Today our maidens gathered here to strew
The carly flowers upon the soldiers' graves,
In their sweet custom; and at early morn
Hither they came with blossoms, buds and leaves,
And earnest faces fairer than the flowers.
No grave has been forgotten-all are dressed.
The simple soldier from the distant State
Is loved and honoured, though perchance unknown,
And where he sleeps is beautiful with bloom.
One stayed a little when the rest were gone
Beside a grave. Quite motionless she stood,
Until the paths grew dim, then turned away;
And twilight gathers over Hollywood.
The sun goes down behind a bank of cloud
And dashes all the stormy west with blood,
As dies a hero in a broken cause,
When, pouring out his wasted life, he leaves
The land he loved to darkness and defeat.
Far down below I hear the river rush,
And standing in this city of the dead,
The voice of waters seems a human cry
That rises from the breadth of all the land
Of shivered hearthstones and of broken hearts.

The city growing sombre in the dusk
Was lit with splendor forty months agone,
When all our best and bravest gathered there,
A nation's fortress and her capital.
The long streets trembled with the tramp of men
And rang with shouting and with martial strains;
And up the glancing river came the boom
Of mighty guns that held a fleet at bay;
But sorrow came upon her and defeat;
She sank in ashes, and a people's hope
Sank with her, and her glory passed away.
Her arms were overthrown, her flag was torn,
Her children bent their heads beneath the yoke
In bitter silence, and her chosen chief
Was fettered in the fortress by the sea.

O rapid river, with the mighty voice,
Rave through thy hills and wear away the rocks,
Even as a people wears away the heart
In thinking on their glory and their fall.
But, oh, the spirit of the first campaigns!
      Oh, days of life and motion!
From Rio Grande to the Chesapeake
They gathered, sweeping joyous to the fight.
The wild yell rising from the tramping charge
Tore through the ragged rifts of battle smoke
And rose above the thunder of the guns;

And as a great wave on the open sea,
That strikes a blow and leaves a wreck behind,
They swept along, a living surge of strength,
With tempest voice and crest of bayonet.
God smiled at first, then turned His face aside,
And hope, that glittered like a sunlit sword,
Was quenched in gloom. And still they smote the foe
That rose, with strength renewed, from each defeat,
Till, broken by their victories, they fell.
For ever thin and thinner grew the ranks,
The weary march, the hungry bivouac,
The scanty blanket, wet with driving sleet,
The sleepless outpost, listlessness of camp,
The longing for the loved at home—all these,
Far more than wasting battle, wasted them,
Until their strength was spent. Now low they lie;
And never more upon Virginia hills
Shall thrill the onset of the Southern lines.
The men who bore the bayonet and the blade
Shall bear them now no more;
But, oh, to think how bright and swift they were,
And now how cold and still!

O rushing river, thou at least art free
And fit to sing a soldier's requiem,
Deep-toned and tremulous-the dirge of men
That once were tameless as thy winter flood.

When once again we stand erect and free,
And we may write a truthful epitaph,
A nation, uttering its grief in stone,
Shall pile aloft a stately monument;
Not that their fame has need of sculptured urn,
For they have lived such lives and wrought such deeds
As venal history cannot lie away.
Till then shall scattered roses deck their graves,
And woman's tear shall be the epitaph.

O river, though they moulder in the dust,
Let them not perish from our hearts. Speak on,
And fill us with thy rushing energy,
That as the gathered freshets of the spring
Burst upward through the shackles of the ice,
So we at last may dash our fetters off,
For until then these men have died in vain.

♦

John Marshall

We are glad to see you, John Marshall, my boy,
    So fresh from the chisel of Rogers;
Go take your stand on the monument there,
    Along with the other old codgers:
With Washington, Jefferson, Henry and such,
Who sinned with a great transgression,
In their old-fashioned notions of freedom and right,
    And their hatred of wrong and oppression.
You come rather late to your pedestal, John,
    Far sooner you ought to have been here;
For the volume you hold is no longer the law,
    And this is no longer Virginia.
The old Marshall-law you expounded of yore
    Is now not at all to the purpose,
And the martial law of the new brigadier
    Is stronger than habeas corpus.
So keep you the volume shut with care,
    For the days of the law are over,
And it needs all your brass to be holding it there
    With "Justice" inscribed on the cover.
Could life awaken the limb of bronze
    And blaze in the burnished eye,

What would ye do with your movement of life,
    Ye men of the days gone by?
Would ye chide us or pity us, blush or weep,
    Ye men of the days gone by?
Would Jefferson tear up the scroll he holds,
That time has proven a lie?
And Marshall shut the volume of law
    And lay it down with a sigh?
Would Mason roll up the Bill of Rights
    From a race unworthy to scan it?
And Henry dash down the eloquent sword
    And clang it against the granite?
And Washington, seated in massy strength
    On the charger that paws the air,
Could he see his sons in their deep disgrace,
    Would he ride so proudly there?
He would get him down from his big brass horse,
    And cover his face at our shame,
For the land of his birth be now "Distriet One,"
    Virginia was once the name!

◆ ◆ ◆

FATHER ABRAM JOSEPH RYAN (1838—1886) was born in Maryland of Irish parents and was a Catholic priest in St. Louis when he joined the Confederate army as a chaplain. During the war he became well-known for his patriotic poems and for tending of the wounded under fire, and for risking himself in heroic service in the deadly epidemics of the time. His younger brother was killed fighting for the Confederacy. Father Ryan wrote this famous poem in the stunning moment of defeat. It is not to be thought that he wished for the flag to be furled forever.

The Conquered Banner

Furl that Banner, for 'tis weary;

Round its staff' tis drooping dreary;

    Furl it, hide it—let it rest!

For there's not a man to wave it,

And there's not a sword to save it,

And there's not one left to lave it

In the blood which heroes gave it;

And its foes now scorn and brave it;

    Furl it, hide it—let it rest!

Take that Banner down! 'tis tattered;

Broken is its staff and shattered;

And the valiant hosts are scattered,

    Over whom it floated high.

Oh, 'tis hard for us to fold it,

Hard to think there's none to hold it,

Hard that those who once unrolled it

    Now must furl it with a sigh!

Furl that Banner-furl it sadly;
Once ten thousands hailed it gladly,
And ten thousands wildly, madly,
   Swore it should forever wave—
Swore that foeman's sword should never
Hearts like theirs entwined dissever,
Till that flag should float forever
   O'er their freedom or their grave!

Furl it! for the hands that grasped it,
And the hearts that fondly clasped it,
   Cold and dead are lying low;
And that Banner—it is trailing,
While around it sounds the wailing
   Of its people in their woe.

For, though conquered, they adore it—
Love the cold, dead hands that bore it!
Weep for those who fell before it!
Pardon those who trailed and tore it!
But, oh, wildly they deplore it,
   Now who furl and fold it so!

Furl that Banner! True, 'tis gory,
Yet 'tis wreathed around with glory,
And 'twill live in song and story
Though its folds are in the dust!
For its fame on brightest pages,
Penned by poets and by sages,
Shall go sounding down the ages—
    Furl its folds though now we must.

Furl that Banner, softly, slowly;
Treat it gently—it is holy,
    For it droops above the dead;
Touch it not—unfold it never;
Let it droop there, furled forever,—
    For its people's hopes are fled.

◆

The Southern Soldier Boy

Young as the youngest who donned the gray,
True as the truest who wore it,
Brave as the bravest he marched away,
(Hot tears on the cheeks of his mother lay);
Triumphant waved our flag one day,
He fell in front before it.

CHORUS—
A grave in the wood with the grass o'er grown,
A grave in the heart of his mother,
His clay in the one lifeless and lone,
But his memory lives in the other.

Firm as the firmest where duty led,
He hurried without a falter;
Bold as the boldest he fought and bled,
And the day was won but the field was red;
And the blood of his fresh young heart was shed,
On his country's hallowed atar.

91

CHORUS—

A grave in the wood with the grass o'er grown,
A grave in the heart of his mother,
His clay in the one lifeless and lone,
But his memory lives in the other.

On the trampled breast of the battle plain,
Where the foremost ranks had wrestled,
The fairest form 'mid all the slain
Like a child asleep he nestled.
In the solemn of the woods that swept
The field where his comrades found him,
They buried him there, and strong men wept,
As in silence they gathered 'round him.

CHORUS—

A grave in the wood with the grass o'er grown,
A grave in the heart of his mother,
His clay in the one lifeless and lone,
But his memory lives in the other.

♦

The Sword of Robert Lee

Forth from its scabbard, pure and bright,
Flashed the sword of Lee!
Far in the front of the deadly fight,
High o'er the brave in the cause of Right
Its stainless sheen, like a beacon light,
Led us to Victory!

Out of its scabbard, where, full long,
It slumbered peacefully,
Roused from its rest by the battle's song,
Shielding the feeble, smiting the strong,
Guarding the right, avenging the wrong,
Gleamed the sword of Lee!

Forth from its scabbard, high in the air
Beneath Virginia's sky—
And they who saw it gleaming there,
And knew who bore it, knelt to swear
That where that sword led they would dare
To follow— and to die!

Out of its scabbard!
Never hand Waved sword from stain as free,
Nor purer sword led braver band,
Nor braver bled for a brighter land,
Nor brighter land had a cause so grand,
Nor cause a chief like Lee!

Forth from its scabbard! How we prayed
That sword might victor be;
And when our triumph was delayed,
And many a heart grew sore afraid,
We still hoped on while gleamed the blade
Of noble Robert Lee!

Forth from its scabbard all in vain
Bright flashed the sword of Lee;
'Tis shrouded now in its sheath again,
It sleeps the sleep of our noble slain,
Defeated, yet without a stain,
Proudly and peacefully!

♦

C. S. A.

Do we weep for the heroes who died for us,
Who living were true and tried for us,
And dying sleep side by side for us;
The Martyr-band
That hallowed our land
With the blood they shed in a tide for us?

Ah! fearless on many a day for us
They stood in front of the fray for us,
And held the foeman at bay for us;
And tears should fall
Fore'er o'er all
Who fell while wearing the Gray for us.

How many a glorious name for us,
How many a story of fame for us
They left: Would it not be a blame for us
If their memories part
From our land and heart,
And a wrong to them, and shame for us?

95

No, no, no, they were brave for us,
And bright were the lives they gave for us;
The land they struggled to save for us
Will not forget
Its warriors yet
Who sleep in so many a grave for us.

On many and many a plain for us
Their blood poured down all in vain for us,
Red, rich, and pure, like a rain for us;
They bleed—we weep,
We live—they sleep,
"All lost," the only refrain for us.

But their memories e'er shall remain for us,
And their names, bright names, without stain for us;
The glory they won shall not wane for us.
In legend and lay
Our heroes in Gray
Shall forever live over again for us.

♦

March of the Deathless Dead

Gather the sacred dust
Of the warriors tried and true,
Who bore the flag of our People's trust
And fell in a cause, though lost, still just
And died for me and you.

Gather them one and all!
From the Private to the Chief,
Come they from hovel or princely hall,
They fell for us, and for them should fall
The tears of a Nation's grief.

Gather the corpses strewn
O'er many a battle plain;
From many a grave that lies so lone,
Without a name and without a stone,
Gather the Southern slain.

We care not whence they came,
Dear in their lifeless clay!
Whether unknown, or known to fame,
Their cause and country still the same—
They died – and wore the Gray.

Wherever the brave had died,
They should not rest apart;
Living, they struggled side by side,
Why should the hand of death divide
A single heart from heart?

Gather their scattered clay,
Wherever it may rest;
Just as they marched to the bloody fray,
Just as they fell on the battle day!
Bury then breast to breast.

The foeman need not dread
This gathering of the brave;
Without sword or flag, with the soundless tread,
We muster once more our deathless dead,
Out of each lonely grave.

The foeman need not frown,
They all are powerless now:
We gather them here and we lay them down,
 And tears and prayers are the only crown
We bring to wreathe each brow.

And the dead thus meet the dead,
While the living o'er them weep:
And the men by Lee and Stonewall led,
And the hearts that once together bled,
Together still shall sleep.

♦

The Land We Love

Land of the gentle and brave!
Our love is as wide as thy woe;
It deepens beside every grave
Where the heart of a hero lies low.

Land of the sunniest skies!
Our love glows the more for thy gloom;
Our hearts, by the saddest of ties
Cling closest to thee in thy doom.

Land where the desolate weep
In a sorrow no voice may console!
Our tears are but streams, making deep
The ocean of love in our soul.

Land where the victor's flag waves,
Where only the dead are free!
Each link of the chain that enslaves,
But binds us to them and to thee.

Land where the Sign of the Cross
Its shadow hath everywhere shed!
We measure our love by thy loss,
Thy loss by the graves of our dead!

♦

A Land Without Ruins

A land without ruins is a land without memories —
a land without memories is a land without history.
A land that wears a laurel crown may be fair to see;
but twine a few sad cypress leaves around
    the brow of any land,
and be that land barren, beautiless and bleak,
    it becomes lovely
in its consecrated coronet of sorrow,
    and it wins the sympathy of the heart
and of history. Crowns of roses fade —
    crowns of thorns endure.
Calvaries and crucifixions take deepest hold
    of humanity —
the triumphs of might are transient —
    they pass and are forgotten —
the sufferings of right are graven deepest on
    the chronicle of nations.

Yes give me the land where the ruins are spread,
And the living tread light on the hearts of the dead;
Yes, give me a land that is blest by the dust,
And bright with the deeds of the down-trodden just.
Yes, give me the land where the battle's red blast
Has flashed to the future the fame of the past;
Yes, give me the land that hath legends and lays
That tell of the memories of long vanished days;
Yes, give me a land that hath story and song!
Enshrine the strife of the right with the wrong!
Yes, give me a land with a grave in each spot,
And names in the graves that shall not be forgot;
Yes, give me the land of the wreck and the tomb;
There is grandeur in graves — there is glory in gloom;
For out of the gloom future brightness is born,
As after the night comes the sunrise of morn;
And the graves of the dead with the grass overgrown
May yet form the footstool of liberty's throne,
And each single wreck in the war path of might
  Shall yet be a rock in the temple of right.

♦ ♦ ♦

JOSEPH BLYTH ALLSTON (1833—1904) of South Carolina, Confederate soldier, was a prisoner of the Yankees at Fort Delaware who wrote this when news of Lee's surrender was received. Allston was the author of *Battle Songs*.

Stack Arms

"Stack Arms!" I've gladly heard the cry
When, weary with the dusty tread
Of marching troops, as night drew nigh
I sank upon my soldier's bed
And calmly slept: the starry dome
Of heaven's blue arch my canopy,
And mingled with my dreams of home
The thoughts and peace of liberty.

''Stack Arms! I've heard it when the shout
Exulting, rang along our line,
Of foes hurled back in bloody rout, Captured,
dispersed; it tones divine, Then came to mine
enraptured ear, Guerdon of duty nobly done,
And glistened on my cheek, the tear Of grateful joy
for victory won.

103

"Stack Arms!" In faltering accents, slow
And sad, it creeps from tongue to tongue,
A broken, murmuring wail of woe,
For manly hearts by anguish wrung:
Like victims of a midnight dream,
We move, we know not how nor why,
For life and hope but phantoms seem,
And it were a relief—to die.

♦ ♦ ♦

CAROLINE AUGUSTA BALL (1825–1900) of South Carolina
was a direct descendant of the Revolutionary patriot John Rutledge.

The Jacket of Gray

Fold it up carefully, lay it aside;

Tenderly touch it, look on it with pride;

For dear to our hearts must it be evermore,

The jacket of gray our loved soldier-boy wore.

Can we ever forget when he joined the brave band

That rose in defense of our dear Southern land,

And in his bright youth hurried on to the fray,

How proudly he donned it — the jacket of gray?

His fond mother blessed him and looked up above,

Commending to Heaven the child of her love;

What anguish was hers mortal tongue cannot say,

When he passed from her sight in the jacket of gray.

But her country had called and she would not repine,

Though costly the sacrifice placed on its shrine;

Her heart's dearest hopes on its altar she lay,

When she sent out her boy in the jacket of gray.

Months passed and wars thunders rolled over the land,

Unsheathed was the sword and lighted the brand;

We heard in the distance the sound of the fray,

And prayed for our boy in the jacket of gray.

Ah, vain, all in vain, were our prayers and our tears,
The glad shout of victory rang in our ears;
But our treasured one on the red battle-field lay,
While the life-blood oozed out of the jacket of gray.

His young comrades found him, and tenderly bore
The cold lifeless form to his home by the shore;
Oh, dark were our hearts on that terrible day,
When we saw our dead boy in the jacket of gray.

Ah! spotted and tattered, and stained now with gore,
Was the garment which once he so proudly wore;
We bitterly wept as we took it away,
And replaced with death's white robes the jacket of gray.

We laid him to rest in his cold narrow bed,
And graved on the marble we placed o'er his head
As the proudest tribute our sad hearts could pay —
"He never disgraced it, the jacket of gray."

Then fold it up carefully, lay it aside,
Tenderly touch it, look on it with pride;
For dear must it be to our hearts evermore,
The jacket of gray our loved soldier boy wore!!

♦ ♦ ♦

W.M. BELL on President Davis in Prison

Calm Martyr of a Noble Cause

Calm martyr of a noble cause,
    Upon thy form in vain
The Dungeon clanks its cankerous jaws,
    And clasps it cankered chain;
For thy free spirit walks abroad,
    And every pulse is stirred
With the old deathless glory thrill,
    Whene'er thy name is heard.

♦ ♦ ♦

"CAPTIVES GOING HOME"

Captives Going Home

No flaunting banners o'er them wave,
No arms flash back the sun's bright ray,
No shouting crowds around them throng,
No music cheers them on their way:
They're going home. By adverse fate
Compelled their trusty swords to sheathe;
True soldiers they, even though disarmed—
Heroes, though robbed of victory's wreath.

Brave Southrons! 'Tis with sorrowing hearts
We gaze upon them through our tears,
And sadly feel how vain were all
Their heroic deeds through weary years;
Yet 'mid their enemies they move
With firm, bold step and dauntless mien:
Oh, Liberty! in every age,
Such have thy chosen heroes been.

Going home! Alas, to them the words
Bring visions fraught with gloom and woe:
Since last they saw those cherished homes

The legions of the invading foe
Have swept them, simoon-like, along,
Spreading destruction with the wind!
"They found a garden, but they left
A howling wilderness behind."

Ah! in those desolated homes
To which the "fate of war has come,"
Sad is the welcome-poor the feast—
That waits the soldier's coming home;
Yet loving ones will round him throng,
With smiles more tender, if less gay,
And joy will brighten pallid cheeks
At sight of the dear boys in gray.

Aye, give them welcome home, fair South,
For you they've made a deathless name;
Bright through all after-time will glow
The glorious record of their fame.
They made a nation. What, though soon
Its radiant sun has seemed to set;
The past has shown what they can do,
The future holds bright promise yet.

◆ ◆ ◆

"THE CONFEDERATE FLAG"

The Confederate Flag

No more o'er human hearts to wave,
Its tattered folds forever furled:
We laid it in an honoured grave,
And left its memories to the world.

The agony of long, long years,
May, in a moment, be compressed,
And with a grief too deep for tears,
A heart may be oppressed.

Oh! there are those who die too late
For faith in God, and Right, and Truth—
The cold mechanic grasp of Fate
Hath crushed the roses of their youth.

More blessed are the dead who fell
Beneath it in unfaltering trust,
Than we, who loved it passing well,
Yet lived to see it trailed in dust.

It hath no future which endears,
And this farewell shall be our last:
Embalm it in a nation's tears,
And consecrate it to the past!

To mouldering hands that to it clung,
And flaunted it in hostile faces,
To pulseless arms that round it flung,
The terror of their last embraces—

To our dead heroes—to the hearts
That thrill no more to love or glory,
To those who acted well their parts,
Who died in youth and live in glory—

With tears forever be it told,
Until oblivion covers all:
Until the heavens themselves wear old,
And totter slowly to their fall.

◆ ◆ ◆

LT. ROBERT FALLIGANT (1839—1902) of Georgia.

Doffing the Gray

Off with your gray suits, boys —
Off with your rebel gear—
They smack too much of the cannon's peal,
The lightning flash of your deadly steel,
The terror of your spear.

Their color is like the smoke
That curled o'er your battle-line;
They call to mind the yell that woke
When the dastard columns before you broke,
And their dead were your fatal sign.

Off with the starry wreath,
Ye who have led our van,
To you 'twas the pledge of glorious death,
When we followed you o'er the gory heath,
Where we whipped them man to man.

Down with the cross of stars—
Too long hath it waved on high;
'Tis covered all over with battle scars,
But its gleam the Northern banner mars
'Tis time to lay it by.

Down with the vows we've made,
Down with each memory—
Down with the thoughts of our noble dead
Down, down to the dust,
Where their forms are laid
And down with Liberty.

♦ ♦ ♦

PAUL HAMILTON HAYNE (1830—1886) of South Carolina. Hayne was a romantic poet whose greatest popularity came after The War. The Yankee bombardment of Charleston destroyed his historic family home and library in Charleston, and he lived thereafter in a cabin in the woods near Augusta, Georgia. Hayne's work appears in previous and later volumes of *Southern Poets and Poems*.

South Carolina to the States of the North

(excerpt)

I lift these hands with iron fetters banded;

Beneath the scornful sunlight and bold stars.

I rear my once imperial forehead branded

By alien shame's immedicable scars....

◆

Sonnet: Carolina

THAT fair young land which gave me birth is dead!
Lost as a fallen star that quivering dies
Down the pale pathway of Autumnal skies,
A vague faint radiance flickering where it fled;
All she hath wrought, all she hath planned or said,
Her golden eloquence, her high emprise,
Wrecked, on the languid shore of Lethe lies,
While cold Oblivion veils her piteous head:
O mother! loved and loveliest! debonair
As some brave Queen of antique chivalries,—
Thy beauty's blasted like thy desolate coasts;—
Where now thy lustrous form, thy shining hair?
Where thy bright presence, thine imperial eyes?
Lost in dim shadows of the realm of Ghosts!

♦

Ode: In Honour of the Bravery and Sacrifices of the Soldiers of the South

Four deadly years we fought,

Ringed by a girdle of unfaltering fire,

That coiled and hissed in lessening circles nigher.

Blood dyed the Southern wave;

From ocean border to calm inland river,

There was no pause, no peace, no respite ever.

Blood of our bravest brave

Drenched in a scarlet rain the western lea,

Swelled the hoarse waters of the Tennessee,

Incarnadined the gulfs, the lakes, the rills,

And from a hundred hills

Steamed in a mist of slaughter to the skies,

Shutting all hope of heaven from mortal eyes.

The Beaufort blooms were withered on the stem;

The fair gulf city in a single night

Lost her imperial diadem;

And wheresoe' er men's troubled vision sought,

They viewed MIGHT towering o'er the humbled

    crest of RIGHT!

Enough! 'tis over! The last gleam of hope

Hath melted from our mournful horoscope,

Of all, of all bereft,

Only to us are left

Our buried heroes and their matchless deeds;

These cannot pass; they hold the vital seeds

Which in some far, untracked, unvisioned hour

May burst to vivid and glorious flower.

Meanwhile, upon the nation's broken heart

Her martyrs sleep. O! dearer far to her,

Than if each son, a wreathed conqueror,

Rode in triumphant state

The loftiest crest of fate;

O! dearer far, because outcast and low,

She yearns above them in her awful woe.

♦

Sonnet

Rise from your gory ashes stern and pale,
Ye martyred thousands and with dreadful ire,
A voice of doom, a front of gloomy fire,
Rebuke those faithless souls, whose querulous wail
Disturbs your sacred sleep — The withering hail
Of battle, hunger, pestilence, despair,
Whatever of mortal anguish man may bear,
We bore unmurmuring! strengthened by the mail
Of a most holy purpose!—then we died!—
Vex not our rest by cries of selfish pain,
But to the noblest measure of your powers
Endure the appointed trial! Griefs defied,
But launch their threatening thunderbolts in vain,
And angry storms pass by in gentlest showers!

◆ ◆ ◆

SIDNEY A. JONAS (d. 1915) of Mississippi. There is considerable controversy about the authorship of "A Confederate Note," probably because copies were found in various places in the South, sometimes written on actual Confederate currency. Major Jonas seems the likeliest author and perhaps wrote the verse on his way home after the surrender.

A Confederate Note

Representing nothing on God's earth now,
And naught in the waters below it—
As the pledge of a nation that's dead and gone,
Keep it, dear friend, and show it.

Show it to those who will lend an ear,
To the tale that this trifle will tell
Of Liberty born of a patriot's dreams,
Of a storm-cradled nation that fell.

Too poor to possess the precious ores,
And too much of a stranger to borrow,
She issued to-day our promise to pay,
And hoped to redeem on the morrow.

We knew it had hardly a value in gold,
Yet as gold our soldiers received it;
It gazed in our eyes with a "promise" to pay,
And each patriot soldier believed it.

Keep it, it tells all our history o'er,
From the birth of our dream to the last—
Modest, and born of the Angel Hope,
Like our hope of success, it passed!

♦

Only a Soldier's Grave

Only a soldier's grave! Pass by,
For soldiers, like other mortals, die.
Parents had he — they are far away;
No sister weeps o'er the soldier's clay;
No brother comes, with tearful eye;
It's only a soldier's grave — pass by.

True, he was loving, and young, and brave,
Though no glowing epitaph honours his grave;
No proud recital of virtues known,
Of griefs endured, or triumphs won;
No tablet of marble, or obelisk high; —
Only a soldier's grave: — pass by.

Yet bravely he wielded his sword in fight,
And he gave his life in the cause of right!
When his hope was high, and his youthful dream
As warm as the sunlight on yonder stream;
His heart unvexed by sorrow or sigh; —
Yet, 'tis only a soldier's grave: – pass by.

121

Yet, we should mark it – the soldier's grave,
Some one may seek him in hope to save!
Some of the dear ones, far away,
Would bear him home to his native clay:
T'were sad, indeed, should they wander,
Find not the hillock, and pass him by.

♦ ♦ ♦

SIDNEY LANIER (1842–1881) of Georgia was talented as a poet and a musician. He served in the Confederate Army and spent the latter part of the War in the notorious Yankee POW camp at Point Lookout, Maryland, which permanently damaged his health and shortened his life. His postwar life was a struggle, although he eventually landed a post as lecturer at Johns Hopkins, which had many Southerners as faculty and students.

Tyranny

Spring-germs, spring-germs
I charge you by your life, go back to death.
This glebe is sick, the wind is foul of breath
Stay: feed the worms.

Oh! Every clod
Is faint, and falters from the war of growth
And crumbles in a dreary dust of sloth,
Unploughed, untrod.

What need, what need,
To hide with flowers the curse upon the hills,
Or sanctify the banks of sluggish rills
Where vapors breed.

And—if needs must —
Advance, O Summer-heats! upon the land,
And bake the bloody mould to shards and sand
And barren dust.

Before your birth,
Burn up, O Roses! in your natal flame.
Good Violets, sweet Violets, hide shame
    Below the earth.

    Ye silent Mills,
Reject the bitter kindness of the moss.
O Farms! protest if any tree emboss
    The barren hills.

    Young Trade is dead,
And swart Work sullen sits in the hillside fern
And folds his arms that find no bread to earn,
    And bows his head.

    Spring-germs, spring-germs,
Albeit the towns have left you place to play,
I charge you, sport not. Winter owns to-day,
    Stay: feed the worms.

♦

The Raven Days

Our hearths are gone out, and our hearts are broken,
    And but the ghosts of homes to us remain,
And ghostly eyes and hollow sighs give token
    From friend to friend of an unspoken pain.

O, Raven Days, dark Raven Days of sorrow,
    Bring to us, in your whetted ivory beaks,
Some sign out of the far land of To-morrow,
    Some strip of sea-green dawn, some orange streaks.

Ye float in dusky files, forever croaking—
    Ye chill our manhood with your dreary shade.
Pale, in the dark, not even God invoking,
    We lie in chains, too weak to be afraid.

O Raven Days, dark Raven Days of sorrow,
    Will ever any warm light come again?
Will ever the lit mountains of To-morrow
    Begin to gleam across the mournful plain?

♦ ♦ ♦

CARLYLE McKINLEY (1847—1904) of South Carolina left the University of Georgia at the age of 15 to join the Confederate army in the defense of Atlanta. After the war he became a prominent staff member of the *Charleston News & Courier*. He wrote the first accounts of the Charleston hurricane of 1885 and earthquake of 1886. His verse appears also in the next volume of *The Land They Loved*.

South Carolina, 1876

Naked and desolate she stands,

Her name a byword in all lands,

Her scepter wrested from her hands.

—She smiles, a queen despite their bands!

Her crown is lying at her feet,

And mockers fill her rulers' seat;

The spoiler's work is near complete.

—Her broad, fair bosom still is sweet!

They've wasted all her royal dower;

They've wrought her wrong with evil power;

And is she faint, or doth she cower?

—She scorns them in her weakest hour!

Her daughters cling about her form,
Their faith and love still high and warm;
They trust in her protecting arm.
—Her dark eyes brood a wrathful storm!

She bides her time a patient Fate!
Her sons are gathering in the gate!
She knows to counsel and to wait
And vengeance knoweth not too late!

◆ ◆ ◆

ALBERT PIKE (1808—1891) of Arkansas appears in the first and second volumes of Southern Poets. "Jubilate" is a celebration of the end of "Reconstruction."

A Lament for Dixie (1868)

Southrons, conquered, subjugated,

Mourn your country devastated!

Mourn for hapless, hopeless Dixie!

Homes once happy, desolated,

Church and altar desecrated;

Mourn for fallen, ruined Dixie!

Lament the fall of Dixie!

Alas! Alas!

On Dixie's land we'll sadly stand,

And live or die for Dixie,

Endure! Endure!

All ills endure for Dixie!

Mourn your dead whose bones lie bleaching,

Courage to the living teaching;

Wail, but still be proud for Dixie!

Mourn your Southland, crushed and trampled,

Bearing sorrows unexampled;

Wail, but still be proud for Dixie!

Prey despoiled and victim bleeding,
Not to man for mercy pleading,
Unto God alone cries Dixie:
Cross of anguish bravely bearing,
 Crown of thorns submissive wearing,
Patient and resigned is Dixie.

All our States lie fainting, dying,
Each to each with sobs replying,
Each still loving, honouring Dixie:
By the accurst scourge lacerated,
By her freed slaves ruled and hated,
She is still our own dear Dixie.

Dear to us our conquered banners,
Greeted once with loud hosannas;
Dear the tattered flag of Dixie;
Dear the field of Honour glorious,
Where, defeated or victorious,
Sleep the immortal Dead of Dixie.

Conquered, we are not degraded,
Southern laurels have not faded;
Mourn, but not in shame, for Dixie!
Deck your heroes' graves with garlands,
Till the echo comes from far lands,
"Honour to the dead of Dixie!"
All is not yet lost unto us,—

Baseness only can undo us;
Mourn—you cannot blush—for Dixie!
Kneeling at your country's altar,
Swear your children not to falter,
Till the right shall rule in Dixie.

If her fate be sealed, we'll share it;
By our shroudless dead we swear it;
Ours the life or death of Dixie!
By her Past's all-glorious story,
By her loyal Martyrs' glory,
We will live or die with Dixie.

Shall there to our Night of Sorrow
Be no glad and bright To-morrow?
Is hope, even, lost to Dixie?—
Every dark night has its morning,
Long though oft, delayed its dawning:
Wait! Be patient! Pray for Dixie!

Hope for dawn for Dixie!
Endure! Endure!
On Dixie's land we'll fearless stand,
And hope and pray for Dixie.
Endure! Endure!
All ills endure for Dixie!

♦

Jubilate

Now our night of terror endeth,
God his Rose of Dawn now sendeth,
   Giving life and light to Dixie:
Arms no longer Fraud sustaining,
Knaves and thieves no longer reigning,
   Hope is once more born for Dixie.
   Life has come to Dixie;
      She's free! free!! free!!!—
On Dixie's land we now may stand,
   No longer tortured Dixie:
     She's free! free!! free!!!
Our own, dear, wasted Dixie:
     She's free! free!! free!!!
For God is good to Dixie.

♦ ♦ ♦

EDMUND RUFFIN (1794—1865) of Virginia has been called "the father of soil science" for his agricultural studies and practice that revitalized the soil of the Southeastern States. He was also a strong secessionist who was allowed in late age to fire the first short in the reduction of Fort Sumter. On 18 June 1865 he ended his own life, leaving the statement:

And now with my latest writing and utterance, and what will near to my latest breath, I hear repeat, & would willingly proclaim, my unmitigated hatred to Yankee rule—to all political, social and business connections with Yankees, & to the perfidious, malignant, & vile Yankee race.

♦ ♦ ♦

WILLIAM GILMORE SIMMS (1806–1870) appears prominently in volumes 1 and 2 of *The Land They Loved*. He passed away in 1870 but made this verse about "Reconstruction."

To Jedediah Quirk, Esq., Politician

Ask not, dear Quirk, with moody brow,
What next the Congress means to do;
Don't bother your brains or mine to know,
   How long the dogs our days decree;
Consult no wizard, nor through Pass,
Of Mesmer, prove yourself an ass,
   And try to make an ass of me!

Better, with Patience, grin and bear,
Than, by the question, rouse the fear
Of worse to come another year,
   While Jove in wrath denies
Season and sky of lengthening bliss;—
Enough that, in a time amiss,
If rightly knowing, using this
   We're, for the Present, wise!

Don't bother with the freedmen, Quirk,
Nor give them rations not to work;
Them, as the Bureau, let us shirk,
    Send both to Jericho.
And don't you seek the President,
With any weather-wise intent,
Of finding out the thing he meant,
    When sneezing months ago.

Quirk, stay at home,— in quiet stay,—
Rack well your wines;—with ice allay;
Ask me to dinner, day by day;
    Live up to all your powers;—
While vexing Thought with future cares,
 And watching Congress, as it swears,—
You know not how the season wears,
    And how your liquor sours!

♦ ♦ ♦

JOHN REUBEN THOMPSON (1823—1873), of Virginia, was a founder and editor of Southern literary magazines, friend and sponsor of Poe. He wrote these lines in 1866 as the U.S. government announced that the great historic Commonwealth of Virginia was now merely Military District No. 1.

Consummatum

Consummatum—the work of destruction is done,
The race of the first of the States has been run,
The guile of her foes finds her triumph at last, And
VIRGINIA, like Poland, belongs to the past.

♦ ♦ ♦

ROBERT BRANK VANCE (1828—1899) of North Carolina was a brother of Governor Zebulon B. Vance. He served as a brigadier general in the Confederate army, commanding the Western North Carolina troops that served in the Army of Tennessee theatre. He was a member of the U.S. House of Representatives 1873—1885 and published several volumes of verse.

The Southern Homes In Ruin

Many a gray-haired sire has died,
As falls the oak, to rise no more,
Because his son, his prop, his pride,
Breathed out his last all red with gore.
No more on earth, at morn, at eve,
Shall age and youth, entwined as one—
Nor father, son, for either grieve
Life's work, alas, for both is done!

Many a mother's heart has bled
While gazing on her darling child,
As in its tiny eyes she read
The father's image, kind and mild;
For ne'er again his voice will cheer
The widowed heart, which mourns him dead;
Nor kisses dry the scalding tear,
Fast falling on the orphan's head!

Many a little form will stray
Adown the glen and o'er the hill,
And watch, with wistful looks, the way
For him whose step is missing still;
And when the twilight steals apace
O'er mead, and brook, and lonely home,
And shadows cloud the dear, sweet face—
The cry will be, "Oh, papa, come!"

And many a home's in ashes now,
Where joy was once a constant guest,
And mournful groups there are, I trow,
With neither house nor place of rest;
And blood is on the broken sill,
Where happy feet went to and fro,
And everywhere, by field and hill,
Are sickening sights and sounds of woe!

There is a God who rules on high,
The widow's and the orphan's friend,
Who sees each tear and hears each sigh,
That these lone hearts to Him may send!
And when in wrath He tears away
The reasons vain which men indite,
The record book will plainest say
Who's in the wrong, and who is right.

◆ ◆ ◆

III. Disbanding

The Confederates have gone out of this war with the proud, secret, deathless, dangerous consciousness that they are THE BETTER MEN.

—Edward Pollard, *The Lost Cause*, 1866

Disbanding The Armies: Farewells

Many of the statements by Confederate commanders to their men on surrender have a moving poetic eloquence. They are too numerous to include in this volume. Michael R. Bradley has made a good collection in his *Last Words: The Farewell Addresses of Union and Confederate Commanders to Their Men.*

NATHAN BEDFORD FORREST (1821—1877). John Allan Wyeth, Confederate cavalryman, wrote that when Forrest's men learned about the decision to surrender "they were overwhelmed with amazement and grief." Some wanted to go to the Trans-Mississppi Dept. to continue the fight, but Forrest said, "what cannot be accomplished here cannot be accomplished in the thinly settled West." In his statement to the men, Forrest over-estimated the magnanimity of the enemy.

Forrest's Farewell to His Men

Headquarters, Cavalry Corps

Gainesville, Alabama,

May 9, 1865

Soldiers:

By an agreement made between Liet. Gen. Taylor, commanding the Department of Alabama. Mississippi, and East Louisiana, and Major-Gen. Canby, commanding United States forces, the troops of this department have been surrendered.

I do not think it proper or necessary at this time to refer to causes which have reduced us to this extremity; nor is it now a matter of material consequence to us how such results were brought about. That we are BEATEN is a self-evident fact, and any further resistance on our part would justly be regarded as the very height of folly and rashness.

The armies of Generals LEE and JOHNSTON having surrendered. You are the last of all the troops of the Confederate States Army east of the Mississippi River to lay down your arms.

The Cause for which you have so long and so manfully struggled, and for which you have braved dangers, endured privations, and sufferings, and made so many sacrifices, is today hopeless. The government which we sought to establish and perpetuate, is at an end. Reason dictates and humanity demands that no more blood be shed. Fully realizing and feeling that such is the case, it is your duty and mine to lay down our arms — submit to the "powers that be" — and to aid in restoring peace and establishing law and order throughout the land.

The terms upon which you were surrendered are favorable, and should be satisfactory and acceptable to all. They manifest a spirit of magnanimity and liberality, on the part of the Federal authorities, which should be met, on our part, by a faithful compliance with all the stipulations and conditions therein expressed. As your Commander, I sincerely hope that every officer and soldier of my command will cheerfully obey the orders given, and carry out in good faith all the terms of the cartel.

Those who neglect the terms and refuse to be paroled, may assuredly expect, when arrested, to be sent North and imprisoned. Let those who are absent from their commands, from whatever cause, report at once to this place, or to Jackson, Miss.; or, if too remote from either, to the nearest United States post or garrison, for parole.

Civil war, such as you have just passed through naturally engenders feelings of animosity, hatred, and revenge. It is our duty to divest ourselves of all such feelings; and as far as it is in our power to do so, to cultivate friendly feelings towards those with whom we have so long contended, and heretofore so widely, but honestly, differed. Neighborhood feuds, personal animosities, and private differences should be blotted out; and, when you return home, a manly, straightforward course of conduct will secure the respect of your enemies.

Whatever your responsibilities may be to Government, to society, or to individuals meet them like men.

The attempt made to establish a separate and independent Confederation has failed; but the consciousness of having done your duty faithfully, and to the end, will, in some measure, repay for the hardships you have undergone.

In bidding you farewell, rest assured that you carry with you my best wishes for your future welfare and happiness.

Without, in any way, referring to the merits of the Cause in which we have been engaged, your courage and determination, as exhibited on many hard-fought fields, has elicited the respect and admiration of friend and foe. And I now cheerfully and gratefully acknowledge my indebtedness to the officers and men of my command whose zeal, fidelity and unflinching bravery have been the great source of my past success in arms.

I have never, on the field of battle, sent you where I was unwilling to go myself; nor would I now advise you to a course which I felt myself unwilling to pursue.

You have been good soldiers, you can be good citizens. Obey the laws, preserve your honour, and the Government to which you have surrendered can afford to be, and will be, magnanimous.

N. B. Forrest, Lieut. General

◆

RANDALL LEE GIBSON (1832—1892) of Louisiana was a Yale graduate and a former attache' to the U.S. embassy in Spain. He was in command of Louisiana troops in major campaigns throughout the war. He later served in the U.S. House and Senate 1875—1892 and was active in promoting education and improvements on the Mississippi River.

Headquarters Gibson's Brigade,
near Meridian, Mississippi,

May 8th, 1865.

Fellow soldiers:

For more than four years we have shared together the fortunes of war.

Throughout all the scenes of this eventful revolution you have been fully tried, and now retire with the consciousness of having achieved a character for discipline, for valour, and for unselfish patriotism, of which you may be justly proud.

There is nothing in your career to look back upon with regret. You have always been in front of the enemy; you have never feasted in soft places at the rear, nor fought your battles at comfortable firesides. Your banners are garlanded with the emblems of every soldierly virtue; more than twenty battle-fields have seen them unfurled; they were never lowered save over the bier of a comrade.

Forget not the good and true men who have fallen. No sculptured marble may perpetuate the memory of their services; but you will wear their names ever green in your hearts, and they will be enshrined forever in the affections of the Southern people, in whose cause they fell.

Comrades! Henceforth other duties will devolve upon you. Adversities can only strengthen the ties that bind you to your country, and increase the obligations you owe to her interests and her honour. As soldiers, you have been amongst the bravest and most steadfast; and as citizens, be law-abiding, peaceable, and industrious.

You have not surrendered, and will never surrender your self-respect and love of country.

You separate not as friends, but brethren, whom common hopes, mutual trials, and equal disasters have made kinsmen.

Hereafter you shall recount to your children with conscious pride the story of these rugged days, and you will always greet a comrade of the old brigade with open arms.

Having commanded a company and regiment in the brigade, I have known many of you from the very beginning of the struggle; have been with you through all its varied fortunes, and offer to each one of you a grateful and affectionate farewell.

May God bless you.

R. L. Gibson, Brigadier-General, Commanding

♦

ROBERT FREDERICK HOKE (1837—1912) of North Carolina. Hoke served throughout the war in VA and NC, rising to Major General in command of a division. He was cited often for outstanding actions. It was said that he would likely be R.E. Lee's successor if needed. After the war he was one of the most admired citizens of his State, was successful in many business enterprises, and refused all temptations to political office.

May 1, 1865
Soldiers of my Division:

On the eve of a long, perhaps final separation, I desire to address to you the last sad words of parting. The fortunes of war have turned the scales against us. The proud banners which you have waved so gloriously on many a field are to be furled at last; but they are not disgraced. My comrades, your indomitable courage, your heroic fortitude, your patience under suffering have surrounded these with a halo which future years cannot dim. History will bear witness to your valour and succeeding generations will point with admiration to your grand struggle for constitutional freedom. Soldiers, your past is full of glory. Treasure it in your hearts.

Remember each gory battlefield, each day of victory, each bleeding comrade. Think then of your future.

Freedom's Battle once begun,

Bequeathed from bleeding sire to son,

Though baffled is oft, is ever won.

You have yielded to overwhelming forces, not to superior valour; you are paroled prisoners, not slaves; the love of liberty, which led you in the contest still burns as brightly in your hearts as ever, cherish it, nourish it, Associate it with the history of the past. Transmit it to your children, teach them the rights of freemen and teach them to maintain them; teach them that the proudest day in all your proud career was that on which you enlisted as a Southern soldier, entering that holy brotherhood whose ties are now sealed in the blood of your compatriots, who have fallen and whose history is covered with the brilliant records of the past four years.

Soldiers, amid the imperishable laurels that now surmount your brows, no brighter leaf adorns you than your late connection with the Army of Northern Virginia. The star that shone with the splendor over its oft repeated field of victory, over the two deadly struggles at Manassas Plains, Richmond, Chancellorsville, and Fredericksburg has sent its rays and been reflected wherever true courage is admired and wherever freedom has a friend. That star has set in blood, but yet in glory. That army is now of the past. Its banners trail, but not with ignominy; no stain blots its escutcheon, no blood can tinge your face as you proudly announce that you have a part in the past history of the Army of Northern Virginia.

My comrades, we have borne together the same hardships, we have braved the same dangers, we have rejoiced over the same victory; your trials and your patience have excited sympathy and admiration and I have borne willing witness to your bravery. It is with a heart full of grateful emotion for your service and ready obedience that I take leave of you.

May the future of every one of you be as happy as your past career has been brilliant and no cloud ever dim the brightness of your fame. The past looms before me in its illuminated grandeur. Its memories are a part of the past life of each of you; but it's all over now. The sad, dark veil of defeat is between us and a life time of sorrow is our only heritage. You carry to your home the heartfelt wishes of your General for your prosperity.

My command, farewell!

R. F. Hoke, Major General
Headquarters, Hoke's Division

(Near Bennett Place, North Carolina)

♦

JOHN SINGLETON MOSBY (1833—1916) of Virginia. Mosby was the partisan leader who effectively harassed the Union occupiers of Northern Virginia.

April 21, 1865

Soldiers! I have summoned you to gather for the last time. The vision we have cherished of a free and independent country has vanished and that country is now the spoil of a conqueror. I disband your organization in preference to surrendering it to our enemies. I am now no longer your commander. After an association of more than two eventful years, I part from you with a just pride in the fame of your achievements and grateful recollections of your generous kindness to myself. And now at this moment of bidding you a final adieu, accept the assurance of my unchanging confidence and regard. Farewell!

◆ ◆ ◆

IV. Memory

Tradition is not the worship of ashes but the preservation of fire.

— Unknown writer

HENRY TIMROD (1828—1867) of South Carolina was well-established as one of America's foremost lyric poets before the war, but the great subject of Southern independence brought forth his best works. Timrod, though suffering from incipient tuberculosis, twice enlisted in the Confederate army but both times was discharged as unfit. Poverty and hardship endured while struggling to support his family in the ruins of Columbia hastened Timrod's death at thirty-nine. A few months before, he had written "The Ode to the Confederate Dead" for the occasion of placing flowers on the Confederate graves at Magnolia Cemetery in Charleston, until then forbidden by the U.S. Army. Some people claim to prefer the vicious and blasphemous "Battle Hymn of the Republic" or Walt Whitman's adolescent jingles, but for my money Timrod's ode is the most magnificent piece of literature to come out of The War. Timrod's verse appears in the previous two volumes of *The Land They Loved*.

Ode to the Confederate Dead
Magnolia Cemetery, Charleston, 1867

Sleep sweetly in your humble graves,

Sleep, martyrs of a fallen cause;

Though yet no marble column craves

The pilgrim here to pause.

In seeds of laurels in the earth

The blossom of your fame is blown,

And somewhere, waiting for its birth,

The shaft is in the stone!

Meanwhile, behalf the tardy years
Which keep in trust your storied tombs,
Behold! your sisters bring their tears,
And these memorial blooms.

Small tributes! but your shades will smile
More proudly on these wreaths to-day,
Than when some cannon-moulded pile
Shall overlook this bay.

Stoop, angels, hither from the skies!
There is no holier spot of ground
Than where defeated valour lies,
By mourning beauty crowned!

♦ ♦ ♦

MARY BAYARD DEVEREUX CLARKE (1827–1886) of North Carolina. This accomplished and versatile poet lived much of the 19th century South in verse—the War, Christian faith, celebration of place. Her work appears not only in this volume but in *The Land They Loved*, Vols. 2 and 4. Along with many others, Mrs. Clarke is proof of the lie that Southern women were discouraged from being intellectual. The first poem in this group observes the death of General Lee in 1870. The third poem of this group was her last and was read by her son at the unveiling of the Confederate monument in New Bern in 1885. "Dux Foemina Facti" concerns the role of women in preserving Confederate memory.

In Memoriam

The conquered banner to the skies

To greet our Jackson rose,

And following now that banner's lead

Our grandest hero goes.

Like some tall mount whose lofty peak

Is first to catch the sun,

And latest to reflect its glow

When closing day is done;

A beacon in our land he stood,

Upon whose noble head,

The earliest and the latest ray,

Of every hope was shed.

He cannot die! On Hist'ry's page
He lives that all may see,
How mortal man erst here below
May yet immortal be.

And to the stars serenely grand
His martyr'd soul takes flight,
That he who was our noontide sun
May thence illume our night.

♦

The Guard Around the Tomb

What is this solemn sound we hear?
It breaks upon a nation's ear
Like Ocean's sob upon the shore,
The wail of storms whose wrath is o'er.
From proud Virginia's mountains grand
It swells through all our Southern land.

A country mourning o'er its slain,
Who gave their lives, and not in vain,
Since in its heart their mem'ry blooms
Fresh as these flowers upon their tombs.
Their toil is o'er, their labors cease.
In war they died, but died for peace.

They bravely fought and nobly fell,
And Fame their glorious deeds shall tell,
When she decrees a crown of bay
No power on earth her hand can stay,
And on these graves a wreath is laid
No storm can change, no time can fade.

Where she has placed this deathless crown
Let woman cast her roses down,
And Love and Fame forever stand
A guard of honour, hand in hand,
Around these graves where heroes lie
Who fought for right nor feared to die.

♦

Dux Foemina Facti

"On Fame's eternal camping ground"
A sentinel now takes his stand,
To guard his comrades' dreamless sleep
Until relieved by Time's command.

But—though this soldier carved in stone
May slowly crumble and decay,—
For "earth to earth and dust to dust"
Material things all pass away:

Yet, Love, like Truth, can never die;
And 'graved on Time's historic page,
The memory of our soldiers' deeds
Shall live undimmed from age to age.

By woman's hand 'tis written there,
"Our dead shall live," she said,
And placed her sentinel above
The grave of the Confederate dead.

Stand there, O effigy in stone!
To guard 'gainst time's corroding dust
The sacred mem'ries of the past
Confided to your silent trust.

♦ ♦ ♦

SAMUEL DAVIS of North Carolina. This poet has not been identified with certainty but the verse indicates that he had been a Confederate soldier at Petersburg.

The Lines Around Petersburg

("Such a sleep they sleep, The men I loved!" – Tennyson)

Oh, silence, silence! now, when night is near,
And I am left alone,
Thou art so strange, so sad reposing here
And all so changed hath grown,
Where all was once exuberant with life
Through day and night, in deep and deadly strife.

If I must weep, oh, tell me, is there not
Some plaintive story breathed into mine ear
By spirit-whispers from the voiceless sphere,
Haunting this awful spot?
To my sad soul, more mutely eloquent
Than words of fame on sculptured monument.

Outspeaks yon crumbling parapet, where lies
The broken gun, the idly rusting ball,
Mute tokens of an ill-starred enterprise!
Rude altars reared for costly sacrifice!
Vast work of hero-hands left in thy fall!

Where are they now, that fearless brotherhood,
Who marshalled here,
That fearful year,
In pain and peril, yet undaunted stood,—
Though Death rode fiercest on the battle-storm
And earth lay strewn with many a glorious form?
Where are they now, who, when the strife was done,
With kindly greeting round the camp-fire met,—
And made an hour of mirth, from triumphs won,
Repay the day's stern toil, where the slow sun had set?

Where are they?—
Let the nameless grave declare,—
In strange unwonted hillocks— frequent seen!
Alas! who knows how much lies buried there!—
What worlds of love, and all that might have been!

The rest are scattered now; we know not where;
And Life to each a new employment brings;
But still they seem to gather round me here,
To whom these places were familiar things!
Wide sundered now, by mountain and by stream,
Once brothers— still a brotherhood they seem;
More firm united, since a common woe
Hath brought to common hopes their overthrow!

Brave souls and true;— in toil and danger tried,—
I see them still as in those glorious years,
When strong, and battling bravely side by side,
All crowned their deeds with praise,
    — and some with tears!
'Tis done! the sword is sheathed; the banner furled,
No sound where late the crashing missile whirled—
The dead alone possess the battle-plain;
The living turn them to life's cares again.

Oh, Silence! blessed dreams upon thee wait;
Here Thought and Feeling open their precious store,
And Memory, gathering from the spoils of Fate
Love's scattered treasures, brings them back once more!
So let me often dream,
As up the bright'ning stream
Of olden Time, thought gently leads me on,
Seeking those better days, lost, lost, alas! and gone!

♦ ♦ ♦

HENRY LYNDEN FLASH (1835—1914) of Louisiana and California was a native of Ohio raised in New Orleans. He was in business in Mobile and Galveston and an already a published poet when he joined the Confederate Army. In 1884 he moved to Los Angeles and was active in the United Confederate Veterans on the West Coast.

The Confederate Flag

Four stormy years we saw it gleam,
A people's hope and then refurled,
Even while its glory was the theme
    Of half the world.

A beacon that with streaming ray
Dazzled a struggling nation's sight—
Seeming a pillar of cloud by day,
    Of fire by night.

They jeer who trembled as it hung,
Comet-like blazoning the sky—
And heroes, such as Homer sung,
    Followed it to die.

It fell—but stainless as it rose,
Martyred, like Stephen, in the strife
Passing, like him, girdled with foes,
From Death to Life.

Fame's trophy! Sanctified with tears—
Planted forever at her portal;
Folded, true: What then? Four short years
Made it immortal!

♦ ♦ ♦

ARMISTEAD CHURCHILL GORDON (1855–1931) of Virginia was a lawyer and for many years Rector of the University of Virginia. He was a prolific poet and the author of 15 works of history. He was the brother of the next poet.

The Garden of Death

Where are they who marched away,
Sped with smiles that changed to tears,
Glittering lines of steel and gray
Moving down the battle's way—
Where are they these many years?

Garlands wreathed their shining swords;
They were girt about with cheers,
Children's lispings, women's words,
Sunshine and the songs of birds—
They are gone so many years.

"Lo! beyond their brave array
Freedom's august dawn appears!"
Thus we said: "The brighter day
Breaks above that line of gray."
Where are they these many years?

All our hearts went with them there,
All our love, and all our prayers;
What of them? How do they fare?
They who went to do and dare,
And are gone so many years?

What of them who went away
Followed by our hopes and fears?
Braver never marched than they,
Closer ranks to fiercer fray.
Where are they these many years?

Borne upon the Spartan shield
Home returned that brave array
From the blood-stained battle-field
They might neither win nor yield;
That is all, and here are they.

That is all. The soft sky bends
O'er them, lapped in earth away;
Her benignest influence lends—
Dews and rains and radiance sends
Down upon them, night and day.

Over them the Springtide weaves
All the verdure of her May;
Past them drift the somber leaves
When the heart of Autumn grieves
O'er their slumbers —What care they?

What care they, who failed to win
Guerdon of that splendid day—
Freedom's day—they saw begin,
But that, 'mid the battle's din,
Faded in eclipse away?

All is gone for them. They gave
All for naught. It was their way
Where they loved. They died to save
What was lost. The fight was brave;
That is all, and here are they.

Is that all? Was Duty naught?
Love, and Faith made blind with tears?
What the lessons that they taught?
What the glory that they caught
From the onward sweeping years?

Here are they who marched away
Followed by our hopes and tears;
Nobler never went than they
To a bloodier, madder fray,
In the lapse of all the years.

Garlands still shall wreathe the swords
That they drew amid our cheers:
Children's lispings, women's words,
Sunshine, and the songs of birds
Greet them here through all the years.

With them ever shall aide
All our love and all our prayers,
"What of them?" The battle's tide
Hath not scathed them. Lo! they ride
Still with Stuart down the years.

"Where are they who went away
Sped with smiles that changed to tears?"
Lee yet leads the lines of gray—
Stonewall still rides down this way,
They are Fame's through all the years!

♦ ♦ ♦

JAMES LINDSAY GORDON (1860—1904) of Virginia became a successful lawyer and public official in New York City. He was celebrated as an orator and toured the North often to speak for Democratic candidates.

"Jim—, of Biloxi"

"Jim—, of Biloxi." That is all.

It is graven into the granite wall

Where the monument rises fair

Into the soft Virginian air

Among a hundred comrades' names,—

Their country's heritage,— and Fame's.

Jim—, of Biloxi. Nothing more.

Naught of his name or his fame is sure,

Save that down where the river ran

And the regiments struggled man to man,

An humble son of the fighting South

Gave his life at the musket's mouth.

Perchance where the Sunflower River flows

By forests of jessamine and rose,

Or where the Gulf Stream washes far

Its tides of blue to the vesper star,

Some one waited with prayers and tears

For Jim—, of Biloxi, these many years.

Life and Name and Cause all lost;
Least and last of the mightiest host
That ever wrote in the blood of men
A dream that will never be dreamed again,
Gone like the strain that the bugle blew,
Jim—, of Biloxi, heaven shelter you!

♦ ♦ ♦

THEOPHILUS HUNTER HILL (1836—1901) of North Car-
olina was a newspaper editor, State Librarian, and prolific poet.
His first book of verse was published in Raleigh in 1861 and was
the first book to be copyrighted under the Confederate States of
America. The verse below was written in 1867 as a memorial to
Confederate dead.

Proemial Stanzas

If aught that I have ever said or sung

May cause one more memorial flower to bloom

Where plaintive harps, on Southern willows hung,

Wail, Memnon-like, amid perpetual gloom;

Where, bowed with bleeding heart and eye of stone,

The South, a nobler Niobe, appears,

Murmurs, with quivering lips, "Thy will be done!"

And seeks relief from agony in tears;

If when her trembling hands, unclasped from prayer,

Begin the light of votive flowers to shed,

Exhaling sweets, illumining the air,

Above the graves of her Confederate dead,

She chance to touch and haply intertwine,
Mid flowers of balmier breath and happier hue,
A daisy or forget-me-not of mine,
That erst, unnoticed, by the wayside grew;

This, this would be far dearer than the meed
Of praise awarded to the festive strain,
Blown from a pipe of Carolina reed,
Which, at your bidding, I awake again!

♦ ♦ ♦

JAMES BARRON HOPE (1827—1887) of Virginia was a member of a prominent Naval family and as a young man made two man-of-war voyages with his grandfather, Commodore Samuel Barron. As a student at the College of William Mary, Hope was wounded in a duel with pistols. He served the Confederacy and after the War was a prominent lawyer and journalist in Norfolk for many years. He was frequently the poet of choice for Virginia ceremonial occasions. His verse appears also in volumes two and four of *The Land They Loved*.

The Cadets at New Market

Their sleep is made glorious,

And dead they're victorious

Over defeat!

Never Lethean billows

Shall roll o'er their pillows,

Red with the feet

Of Mars from the wine press

So bitterly sweet!

Sleeping, but glorious,

Dead in Fame's portal,

Dead, but victorious,

Dead, but immortal!

They gave us great glory,

What more could they give?

They have left us a story,

A story to live—

And blaze on the brows of the State
   like a crown,
While from these grand mountains
   the rivers run down,
While grass grows in graveyards,
   or the Ocean's deep calls,
Their deeds and their glory
   shall fresco these walls.

(Delivered at Virginia Military Institute, 1870)

♦

Mahone's Brigade—A Metrical Address

"In pace decus, in bello presidium." —Tacitus.

Your arms are stacked, your splendid colors furled,
Your drums are still, aside your trumpets laid,
But your dumb muskets once spoke to the world—
And the world listened to Mahone's Brigade.

Like waving plume upon Bellona's crest,
Or comet in red majesty arrayed,
Or Persia's flame transported to the West,
Shall shine the glory of Mahone's Brigade.

Not once, in all those years so dark and grim,
Your columns from the path of duty strayed;
No craven act made your escutcheon dim—
'Twas burnished with your blood, Mahone's Brigade.

Not once on post, on march, in camp, or field,
Was your brave leader's trust in you betrayed,
And never yet has old Virginia's shield
Suffered dishonour through Mahone's Brigade.

Who has forgotten at the deadly Mine,
How our great Captain of great Captains bade
Your General to retake the captured line?
How it was done, you know, Mahone's Brigade.

Who has forgotten how th' undying dead,
And you, yourselves, won that for which Lee prayed?
Who has forgotten how th' Immortal said:
That "heroes" swept that field, Mahone's Brigade?

From the far right, beneath the "stars and bars,"
You marched amain to Bushrod Johnson's aid,
And when you charged an arrow shot by Mars
Went forward in your rush, Mahone's Brigade.

In front stood death. Such task as yours before
By mortal man has rarely been essayed,
There you defeated Burnside's boasted corps,
And did an army's work, Mahone's Brigade.

And those who led you, field, or line, or staff,
Showed they were fit for more than mere parade;
Their motto: "Victory or an epitaph,"
And well they did their part, Mahone's Brigade.

*(Recited at Norfolk Opera House, July 30, 1876,
the twelfth anniversary of the Battle of the Crater,
and second reunion of survivors of Mahone's brigade.)*

◆

An Elegiac Ode

(This poem was written in 1866 at the request of the ladies of
Warren County, North Carolina, for the dedication of a memorial
at the resting place of Robert E. Lee's daughter Annie Carter Lee
who died there in 1862. Hope read the poem in front of a large
gathering attended by Annie's brothers Major Generals G.W.C.
and W.H.F. Lee.)

He chastens us as nations and as men,

He smites us sore until our pride doth yield,

And hence our heroes, each with hearts for ten,

Were vanquished in the field;

And stand to-day beneath our Southern sun

O'erthrown in battle and despoiled of hope,

 Their drums all silent and their cause undone,

And they all left to grope

In darkness till God's own appointed time

In His own manner passeth fully by.

Our Penance this. His Parable sublime

Means we must learn to die.

Not as our soldiers died beneath their flags,

Not as in tumult and in blood they fell,

When from their columns, clad in homely rags,

Rose the Confederate yell.

Not as they died, though never mortal men
Since Tubal Cain first forged his cruel blade
Fought as they fought, nor ever shall agen
Such Leader be obeyed!

No, not as died our knightly, soldier dead,
Though they, I trust, have found above surcease
For all life's troubles, but on Christian bed
Should we depart in peace,

Falling asleep like those whose gentle deeds
Are governed through time's passions and its strife,
So justly that we might erect new creeds
From each well ordered life,

Whose saintly lessons are so framed that we
May learn that pain is but a text sublime,
Teaching us how to learn at Sorrow's knee
To value things of time.

Thus thinking o'er life's, promise-breaking dreams,
Its lights and shadows made of hopes and fears,
I say that Death is kinder than he seems,
And not the King of Tears.

♦

The Lee Memorial Ode
(excerpts)

As a soldier we all knew him
Great in action and repose,
Saw how his genius kindled
And his mighty spirit rose
When the four quarters of the globe
Encompassed him with foes.

But he and his grew braver
As the danger grew more rife,
Avaricious they of glory
But most prodigal of life,
And the "Army of Virginia"
Was the Atlas of the strife.

As his troubles gathered round him,
Thick as waves that beat the shore,
Atra Cura rode behind him,
Famine's shadow filled his door;
Still he wrought deeds no mortal man
Had ever wrought before.

•••

III

Then stand up, oh my Countrymen!
And unto God give thanks,
On mountains, and on hillsides
And by sloping river banks—
Thank God that you were worthy
Of the grand Confederate ranks:

That you who came from uplands
And from beside the sea,
Filled with love of Old Virginia
And the teachings of the free,
May boast in sight of all men
That you followed Robert Lee.

Peace has come. God give his blessing
On the fact and on the name!
The South speaks no invective
And she writes no word of blame;
But we call all men to witness
That we stand up without shame.

Nay! Send it forth to all the world
That we stand up here with pride,
With love for our living comrades

And with praise for those who died:
And in this manly frame of mind
Till death we will abide.

God and our consciences alone
Give us measure of right and wrong;
 The race may fall unto the swift
And the battle to the strong:
But the truth will shine in history
And blossom into song.

Human grief full oft by glory
Is assuaged and disappears
When its requiem swells with music
Like the shock of shields and spears,
And its passion is too full of pride
To leave a space for tears.

And hence to-day, my Countrymen,
We come, with undimmed eyes,
In homage of the hero Lee,
The good, the great, the wise!
And at his name our hearts will leap
Till his last old soldier dies.

...

V

When the effigy of Washington
In its bronze was reared on high
'Twas mine, with others, now long gone,
Beneath a stormy sky,
To utter to the multitude
His name that cannot die.

And here to-day, my Countrymen,
I tell you Lee shall ride
With that great "rebel" down the years
Twin "rebels" side by side! —
And confronting such a vision
All our grief gives place to pride.

Those two shall ride immortal
And shall ride abreast of Time,
Shall light up stately history
And blaze in Epic Rhyme
Both patriots, both Virginians true,
Both "rebels," both sublime!

Our past is full of glories
It is a shut-in sea,
The pillars overlooking it
Are Washington and Lee:
And a future spreads before us,
Not unworthy of the free.

And here and now, my Countrymen,
Upon this sacred sod,
Let us feel: It was "Our Father"
Who above us held the rod,
And from hills to sea
Like Robert Lee
Bow reverently to God.

♦

Our Heroic Dead

That past is now like an Arctic Sea
Where the living currents have ceased to run,
But over that past the fame of Lee
Shines out as the "Midnight Sun:"
And that glorious Orb, in its march sublime,
Shall gild our graves till the end of time!

♦

The Future Historian

In the future some historian shall come forth
   both strong and wise,
With a love of the Republic, and the truth,
   before his eyes.
He will show the subtle causes of the war
   between the States,
He will go back in his studies far beyond
   our modern dates,
He will trace out hostile ideas as the miner
   does the lodes,
He will show the different habits born
   of different social codes,
He will show the Union riven,
   and the picture will deplore,
He will show it re-united and made
   stronger than before.
Slow and patient, fair and truthful
   must the coming teacher be
To show how the knife was sharpened
   that was ground to prune the tree.
He will hold the Scales of Justice,
   he will measure praise and blame,
And the South will stand the verdict,
   and will stand it without shame.

◆ ◆ ◆

INSCRIPTION FOR THE SAM DAVIS MONUMENT. As may be seen by the inscriptions, this monument in the Capitol Park in Nashville contained more than a hint of sectional reconciliation. On one side is a poem provided by the New York writer Ella Wheeler Wilcox (1850—1919). Efforts to destroy the statue have been constant. Another Nashville statue of Sam Davis, representing loyalty and bravery, was removed from an academy in 2020.

[Front]

SAM DAVIS

1842   1863

"The Boys Will Have To Fight

The Battles Without Me."

He Gave All He Had—

Life;

He Gained All He Lacked—

Immortality.

This Monument is erected

By contributions from citizens

Of every State in the American Union,

On the site authorized

By the 51st General Assembly

Of the State of Tennessee.

1909

[Rear]
When the Lord calls up earth's heroes,
To stand before His face,
O, many a name, unknown to fame
Shall ring from that high place;
Then out of a grave in the Southland
At the just God's call and beck,
Shall one man rise with fearless eyes
With a rope about his neck;
O Southland! bring your laurels,
And add your wreath, O North!
Let glory claim the hero's name
And tell the world his worth.
— Ella Wheeler Wilcox.

♦♦♦

ROME, GEORGIA, CONFEDERATE MONUMENT

Rome, Georgia:
Confederate Monument Inscription

This monument is the testimony of the present to the future that these were they who kept the faith as it was given them by the fathers. Be it known by this token that these men were true to the traditions of their lineage. Bold, generous, and free, firm in conviction of the right, ready at their country's call, steadfast in their duty, faithful even in despair, and illustrated in the unflinching heroism of their deaths, the freeborn courage of their lives. How well they served their faith, their people know; a thousand battlefields attest; dungeon and hospital bear witness. To their sons they left but honour and their country. Let this stone forever warn those who keep these valleys that only their sires are dead; the principles for which they fought can never die.

(This monument, dedicated in 1910, was badly damaged and removed during the cultural cleansing of the 2020s decade.)

◆ ◆ ◆

JAMES RYDER RANDALL (1839—1908) was a Maryland native who had, like so many other Southerners, moved west, to Louisiana. His best known verse is "Maryland, My Maryland" (*Confederate Poets 1*), written at the very beginning of The War in hope that Maryland would be able to follow Virginia into the Confederacy. Unfortunately, Lincoln's military coup d'etat prevented Marylanders from making a free decision.

Memorial Day

Noblest of martyrs in a glorious fight!
Ye died to save the cause of Truth and Right.
And though your banner beams no more on high,
Not vainly did it wave or did ye die!

No blood for freedom shed is spent in vain;
It is as fertile as the Summer rain;
And the last tribute of heroic breath
Is always conqueror over Wrong and Death.

The grand procession of avenging years
Has turned to triumph all our bitter tears;
And the cause lost, by battle's stern behest,
Is won by Justice, and by Heaven blest.

Dark grew the night above our sacred slain,
Who sleeps upon the mountain and the plain;
But darker still the black and blinding pall
That whelmed the living in its lurid thrall.

But taught by heroes, who had yielded life,
We fainted not, nor faltered in the strife;
With weapons bright, from peaceful Reason won,
We cleaved the clouds and gained the golden sun.

And so today the marble shaft may soar
In memory of those who are no more;
The proudest boast of centuries shall be,
That they who fell with Jackson rise with Lee!

◆ ◆ ◆

AUGUSTUS JULIAN REQUIER (1825—1887) of Alabama was a Mobile attorney.

Ashes of Glory

FOLD up the gorgeous silken sun,
By bleeding martyrs blest,
And heap the laurels it has. won
Above its place of rest.

No trumpet's note need harshly blare
No drum funereal roll—
Nor trailing sables drape the bier
That frees a dauntless soul!

It lived with Lee, and decked his brow
From Fate's empyreal Palm:
It sleeps the sleep of Jackson now—
As spotless and as calm.

It was outnumbered—not outdone;
And they shall shuddering tell,
Who struck the blow, its latest gun
Flashed ruin as it fell.

Sleep, shrouded Ensign! not the breeze
That smote the victor tar,
With death across the heaving seas
Of fiery Trafalgar;

Not Arthur's knights, amid the gloom
Their knightly deeds have starred;
Nor Gallic Henry's matchless plume,
Nor peerless-born Bayard;

Not all that antique fables feign,
And Orient dreams disgorge;
Nor yet, the Silver Cross of Spain,
And Lion of St. George,

Can bid thee pale! Proud emblem,
still Thy crimson glory shines
Beyond the lengthened shades that fill
Their proudest kingly lines.

Sleep! in thine own historic night,—
And be thy blazoned scroll,
A warrior's Banner takes its flight,
To greet the warrior's soul!

♦ ♦ ♦

MERIWETHER "JEFF" THOMPSON (1826—1876), The Confederacy's Missouri "Swamp Fox," was a prolific poet. These untitled verses appear in his memoirs.

After the War

I am sitting here tonight, friend,

The last night of the year—

And am thinking of the gloomy past,

And all the friends so dear

Who have fallen in the horrid war

Which recently scourged our land;

And I mourn for them, the noble dead,

Of our chivalrous Southern band.

For years we marched, for months we stood

    beneath the battle smoke,

And hunger, cold, and sickness faint,

    would hearts less true have broke,

But cheerfully we bore it all;

    and went down, one by one,

Each hoping, as he gave his life,

    your freedom had been won.

And now we stand, a glorious host,

    in our home above the clouds,

And the ragged soldiers from the ditch
　　have sunbeams for their shrouds;
Rough, bearded men, and fair haired boys,
　　are clothed alike in beauty,
For all have died at honour's post;
　　each one has done his duty.

♦ ♦ ♦

FRANCIS ORRAY TICKNOR (1822—1876) of Georgia was a highly regarded physician trained in Philadelphia and a contributor of scientific articles to agricultural publications. He was already established as a poet before the War. He also wrote some of the most memorable Confederate poetry which appears in *The Land They Loved: Vol 2 Confederate Poets and Poems Vol. 1*. His "Little Giffen" is among the greatest verses to come out of the Confederacy.

Dixie

(Air—"Annie Laurie")

Oh! Dixie's homes are bonnie,

And Dixie's hearts are true;

And 'twas down in dear old Dixie

Our life's first breath we drew;

And there our last we'd sigh,

And for Dixie, dear old Dixie,

We'll lay us down and die.

No fairer land than Dixie's

Has ever seen the light;

No braver boys than Dixie's

To stand for Dixie's right.

With hearts so true and high,

And for Dixie, dear old Dixie,

To lay them down and die.

Oh! Dixie's vales are sunny,
And Dixie's hills are blue;
And Dixie's skies are bonnie,
And Dixie's daughters, too,
As stars in Dixie's sky;
And for Dixie, dear old Dixie,
We'd lay us down and die.

No more upon the mountain,
No longer by the shore—
The trumpet song of Dixie
Shall shake the world no more;
For Dixie's songs are o'er,
Her glory gone on high,
And the brave who bled for Dixie
Have laid them down to die.

♦

In Memoriam

Thomas Maduit Nelson, Etat 71

They fail from council and from camp,
   they are falling one by one,
Those grand old heroes of the stamp
   of God-loved Washington;
The task is wrought of mighty minds,
   their glorious day is done,
And Freedom mourns a faded star
   with every setting sun.
The massive brow, the kindly hand,
   the proud and stalwart form
That stood as beacons in the night,
   as bulwarks in the storm.
Ah! few and far on Glory's slope
   their lessening numbers stand,
"The Pillars of a People's hope,"
   the Titans of the land.
The mould is broken; here no more
   those regal souls we meet
Who kept their honour, tho' the world
   had rocked beneath their feet;
The calm, clear dignity that shone
   no clearer for renown,

The matchless majesty that won,
    but would not wear a crown.
Ah! when descends the sullen night
    of Freedom's darkest hour,
When Demagogue and Parasite
    defile the seats of power,
When dust is on the eagle's crest,
    and stain on stripe and star,
Ah! who shall fill their robes in peace,
    or lift their swords in war?
One more to that immortal band,
    that long illustrious line,
That counts no nobler name,
    old friend, or purer soul than thine;
Yea, with the mighty in their death,
    their rest, and their reward,
Sleep, in thy cloudless Fame and Faith,
    true soldier of the Lord.
Sleep with the mighty in thy death!
    yet not with these alone;
Sleep with the loving hearts
    that beat so truly to thine own.
Sleep with the sword-cross on thy breast,
    the well-worn scabbard by,
Fit symbols of a soldier's rest
    and his reward on high.

♦

The Caucasian

Chained to the icy peak,
Rent by the vulture's beak,
Scourged of the bitter brine;
Brother of Caucasus,
The gods have wrought on us
Horrors to rival thine!
In the wilderness wreck we stand,
In the depths of the desolate land,
To our dead in their graves we cry:
"Brothers! that rest in peace
In the land where the wicked cease,
Is it better to live or die?"
And our dead from their graves reply:
"The Merciful moves on high.
The arm of his strength is nigh,
In the sorrows that learn of Faith
To smile in the eye of Death.
It is braver to live than to die!"

♦

Georgia

Between her rivers and beside the sea,
My mother-land! What fairer land can be?

The lyric rapture in her leaping rills,
The crown-imperial on her purple hills.

Her lips are pure that never breathed a curse;
Her hands are white before the universe.

Behold the witness of the King of Peace
Clear, in the splendor of her dew-lit fleece.

And lo! the midnight of her shrouded mine
Garners the radiance of the years to shine.

Yea! the swart Gnome that bides his time below
Shall rise at last, in full regalia glow!

And the great Alchemist shall teach the Sun
That Earth's great gloom and Life's great light are one!

Oh, sweetest souls that ever rose by prayer
White from the furnace-dungeon of despair!

That wrought new grace from battle's chaos mould,
And reared new shrines from ashes not yet cold.

Not cold!—from flames the strangest that have given
From all this world, an altar-smoke to Heaven!

Crowned on the cross, above high-fetter line,
They smile on hate with Love's own smile divine.

Prouder than hills that plume thy star-ward crest,
Sweeter than dales that dimple at thy breast.

Richer than Rome! when God's great chariot rolls,
Imperial Georgia! count thy children's souls.

◆ ◆ ◆

WILLIAM HENRY TRESCOT (1822–1898) of South Carolina was the first historian of American diplomacy and held important posts in the U.S. State Department before The War and again after Reconstruction. During The War he served unofficially in South Carolina's governing counsels. His prose-poem inscription for the Confederate soldiers' monument at the State Capitol in Columbia is among the finest of many of its kind.

Inscription for the Confederate Soldiers' Monument
Columbia, South Carolina

(North Face)

This Monument

Perpetuates the memory

of those who

True to the instincts of their birth,

Faithful to the teachings of their fathers,

Constant in their Love for the State,

Died in performance of their duty;

Who

Have glorified a fallen cause

By the simple manhood, of their lives,

The patient endurance of suffering

And the heroism of death;

and who

In the dark hours of imprisonment,

In the hopelessness of the hospital,

In the short sharp agony of the field,

Found support and consolation

In the belief

That at home they would not be forgotten.

Those for whom they died

Inscribe on this marble

The solemn record of their sacrifice,

The perpetual gratitude of the State they served,

The undying affection of those whose lives

The separation of death

Has shadowed with an everlasting sorrow;

Scattered over the battlefields of the South,

Buried in remote and alien graves,

Dying unsoothed by the touch

Of familiar and household hands,

Their names are here

To recall

To their children and kinsmen

How worthily they lived

How nobly they died;

And in what tender reverence

Their memory survives.

(South Face)

Let the stranger
Who may in future times
Read this inscription,
Recognise that these were men
Whom power could not corrupt,
Whom death could not terrify,
Whom defeat could not dishonour;
And let their virtues plead for just judgment
Of the Cause in which they perished;
Let the South Carolinian
Of another generation
Remember
That the State taught them
How to live and how to die;
And that from her broken fortunes
She has preserved for her children
The priceless treasure of their memories
Teaching all
Who may claim the same birth-right
That Truth, Courage, and Patriotism
Endure forever.

♦ ♦ ♦

MORTON BRYAN WHARTON, D.D. (1839—1908) was a prominent Baptist preacher serving in pulpits all over the South, and the author of numerous very popular books about the Bible. He was born in Virginia, but lived primarily in Eufaula, Alabama. He was converted in 1860, assisted Confederate army chaplains, and later was well-educated and travelled in Europe.

The Death of Jefferson Davis

Our mighty Chieftain breathes no more,
    His noble form, now cold and still,
Has fallen at last, life's conflict o'er,
    Obedient to his Maker's will.
As die the brave and true, he dies,—
    He rests upon a stainless shield,
The great Commander of the skies
    Alone could call him from the field.

His noble spirit dwells on high,
    Where slanders never vex the soul;
And fitting tis his dust should lie
    Far, far removed from prowling ghoul.
Among his friends should be his tomb,
    There on old Ocean's utmost verge,
Where snow-white flowers perennial bloom
    And wild waves chant his funeral dirge.

And he will stand on History's page,
> While cycling years shall onward move,
The victim once of senseless rage,
> Now, idol of his people's love.
When hate is buried in the dust,
> When party strife shall break its spear,
When truth is free and men are just,
> Then will his epitaph appear.
The Parian quarry asks for time
> In which the marble to mature,
Destined to speak his fame sublime,
> Worthy to shrine a heart so pure;
Till then unmarked we bid him lay,
> With carping critics plead a truce,
But dear the spot which holds his clay
> As that which holds the heart of Bruce.

◆ ◆ ◆

SAMUEL ELLIOTT WHITE (1837—1911) of South Carolina. In 1895 White erected at Fort Mill, South Carolina, a marble monument "To the Faithful Slaves" of the Confederacy. The east side of the monument carries a carved image of an African-American man and the west side a similar image of an African-American woman with a baby. The other sides have inscriptions:

[On the North Side]

1895

Erected by Sam'l E. White,

In grateful Memory of Earlier

Days, with Approval of the

Jefferson Davis

Memorial Association.

Among the Many Faithful,

Nelson White	Anthony White
Sandy White	Jim White
Warren White	Henry White
Silas White	Nathan Springs
Handy White	Soloman Spratt

[On the South Side]

1860

Dedicated to

The Faithful Slaves

Who, loyal to a sacred trust,

Toiled for the Support

Of the Army, with Matchless

Devotion, and with Sterling

Fidelity Guarded Our Defenceless

Homes, Women, and Children,

During The Struggle for the Principles

Of Our "Confederate States of

America."

1865

♦ ♦ ♦

DANIEL BEDINGER LUCAS (1836—1909) of Virginia was a lawyer, orator, legislator, and judge. He served in the Confederate Army for a time early in the war but was released due to a childhood spinal injury. In early 1865 he ran the blockade to get to Canada and thence to New York to be the defense attorney for Capt. John Yeats Beall who was executed by the Yankees as a spy. This verse was first published in Montreal. We end the book with this profound meditation on the Confederate experience.

In the Land Where We Were Dreaming

FAIR were our visions! Oh, they were as grand

As ever floated out of Faerie land;

Children were we in single faith,

But God-like children, whom, nor death,

Nor threat, nor danger drove from Honour's path—

In the land where we were dreaming.

Proud were our men, as pride of birth could render;

As violets, our women pure and tender;

And when they spoke, their voice did thrill

Until at eve, the whip-poor-will,

At morn the mocking-bird, were mute and still

In the land where we were dreaming.

And we had graves that covered more of glory

Than ever tracked tradition's ancient story;

And in our dream we wove the thread

Of principles for which had bled
And suffered long our own immortal dead
In the land where we were dreaming.

Tho' in our land we had both bond and free,
Both were content; and so God let them be;—
'Till envy coveted our land
And those fair fields our valour won:
But little recked we, for we still slept on,
In the land where we were dreaming.

Our sleep grew troubled and our dreams grew wild;
Red meteors flashed across our heaven's field;
Crimson the moon; between the Twins
Barbed arrows fly, and then begins
Such strife as when disorder's Chaos reigns,
In the land where we were dreaming.

Down from her sun-lit heights smiled Liberty
And waved her cap in sign of Victory—
The world approved, and everywhere
Except where growled the Russian bear,
The good, the brave, the just gave us their prayer
In the land where we were dreaming.

We fancied that a Government was ours—
We challenged place among the world's great powers;
We talked in sleep of Rank, Commission,

Until so life-like grew our vision,
That he who dared to doubt but met derision
In the land where we were dreaming.

We looked on high: a banner there was seen,
Whose field was blanched and spotless in its sheen—
Chivalry's cross its Union bears,
 And vet'rans swearing by their scars
Vowed they would bear it through a hundred wars
In the land where we were dreaming.

A hero came amongst us as we slept;
At first he lowly knelt—then rose and wept;
Then gathering up a thousand spears
He swept across the field of Mars;
Then bowed farewell and walked beyond the stars—
In the land where we were dreaming.

We looked again: another figure still
Gave hope, and nerved each individual will—
Full of grandeur, clothed with power,
Self-poised, erect, he ruled the hour
With stern, majestic sway—of strength a tower
In the land where we were dreaming.

As, while great Jove, in bronze, a warder God,
Gazed eastward from the Forum where he stood,
Rome felt herself secure and free,

So, "Richmond's safe," we said, while we
Beheld a bronzed Hero God-like Lee,
In the land where we were dreaming.

As wakes the soldier when the alarum calls
As wakes the mother when the infant falls
As starts the traveller when around
His sleeping couch the fire-bells sound—
So woke our nation with a single bound
In the land where we were dreaming.

Woe! woe is me! the startled mother cried—
While we have slept our noble sons have died!
Woe! woe is me! how strange and sad,
That all our glorious vision's fled
And left us nothing real but the dead
In the land where we were dreaming.

And are they really dead, our martyred slain?
No! dreamers! morn shall bid them rise again
From every vale—from every height
On which they seemed to die for right—
Their gallant spirits shall renew the fight
In the land where we were dreaming.

♦ ♦ ♦

About the Editor

DR. CLYDE N. WILSON is Emeritus Distinguished Professor of History of the University of South Carolina, where he served from 1971 to 2006. He holds a Ph.D. from the University of North Carolina at Chapel Hill. He recently completed editing of a 28-volume edition of *The Papers of John C. Calhoun* which has received high praise for quality. He is author or editor of more than 40 other books and over 750 articles, essays, and reviews in a variety of books and journals, and has lectured all over the U.S. and in Europe, many of his lectures having been recorded online and on CDs and DVDs. Dr. Wilson directed 17 doctoral dissertations, a number of which have been published. His books written or edited include *Why the South Will Survive, Carolina Cavalier: The Life and Mind of James Johnston Pettigrew, The Essential Calhoun*, three volumes of *The Dictionary of Literary Biography on* American Historians, *From Union to Empire: Essays in the Jeffersonian Tradition, Defending Dixie: Essays in Southern History and Culture, Chronicles of the South, Calhoun: A Statesman for the 21st Century, The Yankee Problem, African American Slavery in Historical Perspective,* and *Looking For Mr. Jefferson.* Dr. Wilson is founding director of the Society of Independent Southern Historians; former president of the St. George Tucker Society for Southern Studies; recipient of the Bostick Prize for Contributions to South Carolina Letters, the first annual John Randolph Society Lifetime Achievement Award, and of the Robert E. Lee Medal of the Sons of Confederate Veterans. He is M.E. Bradford Distinguished Professor of the Abbeville Institute; Contributing Editor of *Chronicles: A Magazine of American Culture*; founding dean of the Stephen D. Lee Institute, educational arm of the Sons of Confederate Veterans; and co-founder of Shotwell Publishing.

Dr. Wilson lives in the Dutch Fork of South Carolina, not far from the Santee Swamp where Francis Marion and his men rested between raids on the first invader.

THE SOUTH'S FINEST CONTEMPORARY AUTHORS.

Shotwell Publishing is proud to be called home by many of today's most respected Southern scholars and literary greats.

JEFFERY ADDICOTT
Union Terror: Debunking the False Justifications for Union Terror

Trampling Union Terror: Riders of the Second Alabama Cavalry

MARK ATKINS
Women in Combat: Feminism Goes to War

JOYCE BENNETT
Maryland, My Maryland: The Cultural Cleansing of a Small Southern State

GARRY BOWERS
Slavery and The Civil War: What Your History Teacher Didn't Tell You

Dixie Days: Reminiscences Of a Southern Boyhood

The Ultimate Primer for the Southern Outdoorsman

JERRY BREWER
Dismantling the Republic

ANDREW P. CALHOUN
My Own Darling Wife: Letters From A Confederate Volunteer

JOHN CHODES
Segregation: Federal Policy or Racism?

Washington's KKK: The Union League During Southern Reconstruction

WALTER BRIAN CISCO
War Crimes Against Southern Civilians

DAVID T. CRUM
Stonewall Jackson: Saved by Providence

STEPHEN DAVIS
Confederate Triumph: How the South Won Its War for Independence 1861-1863 Volume One:1861

JOHN DEVANNY
Continuities: The South in a Time of Revolution

Lincoln's Continuing Revolution: Essays of M.E. Bradford and Thomas H. Landess

JOSHUA DOGGRELL
Doxed: The Political Lynching of a Southern Cop

JAMES C. EDWARDS
What Really Happened?: Quantrill's Raid On Lawrence, Kansas

TED EHMANN
Boom & Bust In Bone Valley: Florida's Phosphate Mining History 1886-2021

JOHN AVERY EMISON
The Deep State Assassination of Martin Luther King Jr.

DON GORDON
Snowball's Chance: My Kidneys Failed, My Wife Left Me & My Dog Died...

JOHN R. GRAHAM
Constitutional History of Secession

PAUL C. GRAHAM
Confederaphobia

When The Yankees Come: Former Carolina Slaves Remember

Nonsense on Stilts: The Gettysburg Address & Lincoln's Imaginary Nation

JOE D. HAINES
*The Diary of Col. John Henry Stover Funk
of the Stonewall Brigade, 1861-1862*

CHARLES HAYES
The REAL First Thanksgiving

V.P. HUGHES
Col. John Singleton Mosby: In the News 1862-1916

TERRY HULSEY
25 Texas Heroes

*The Constitution of Non-State Government:
Field Guide to Texas Secession*

JOSEPH JAY
*Sacred Conviction:
The South's Stand for Biblical Authority*

JAMES R. KENNEDY
Dixie Rising: Rules For Rebels

*Nullifying Federal and State Gun Control:
A How-To Guide For Gun Owners*

*When Rebel Was Cool:
Growing Up In Dixie, 1950-1965*

*Reconstruction: Destroying the Republic
and Creating an Empire*

Uncle Seth Fought the Yankees: Book 1

WALTER D. KENNEDY
The South's Struggle: America's Hope

*Lincoln, The Non-Christian President:
Exposing The Myth*

Lincoln, Marx, and the GOP

J.R. & W.D. KENNEDY
*Jefferson Davis: High Road to Emancipation
and Constitutional Government*

*Yankee Empire:
Aggressive Abroad and Despotic at Home*

Punished With Poverty: The Suffering South

The South Was Right! 3rd Edition

LEWIS LIBERMAN
Snowflake Buddies; ABC Leftism For Kids!

PHILIP LEIGH
*The Devil's Town: Hot Springs During
The Gangster Era*

U.S. Grant's Failed Presidency

The Causes of the Civil War

*The Dreadful Frauds: Critical Race Theory
And Identity Politics*

JACK MARQUARDT
*Around The World In 80 Years: Confessions
of a Connecticut Confederate*

MICHAEL MARTIN
Southern Grit: Sensing The Siege at Petersburg

SAMUEL MITCHAM
*The Greatest Lynching In American History:
New York, 1863*

*Confederate Patton: Richard Taylor and
The Red River Campaign*

CHARLES T. PACE
Lincoln As He Really Was

*Southern Independence. Why War? The War
To Prevent Southern Independence*

JAMES R. ROESCH
From Founding Fathers To Fire Eaters

KIRKPATRICK SALE
*Emancipation Hell: The Tragedy Wrought
By Lincoln's Emancipation Proclamation*

JOSEPH SCOTCHIE
*The Asheville Connection:
The Making of a Conservative*

*Samuel T. Francis and
Revolution from the Middle*

Green Altar (Literary Imprint)

CATHARINE SAVAGE BROSMAN
*An Aesthetic Education
and Other Stories (2nd Ed)*

Chained Tree, Chained Owls: Poems

Aerosols and Other Poems

Partial Memoirs

RANDALL IVEY
*A New England Romance:
and Other Southern Stories*

The Gift of Gab

SUZANNE JOHNSON
Maxcy Gregg's Sporting Journals 1842-1858

JAMES E. KIBLER, JR.
Tiller : Claybank County Series, Vol. 4

The Gentler Gamester

*Beyond The Stone: Poems of Tribute
& Remembrance*

THOMAS MOORE
*A Fatal Mercy:
The Man Who Lost The Civil War*

PERRIN LOVETT
The Substitute, Tom Ironsides 1

Judging Athena

KAREN STOKES
Belles

Carolina Twilight

Honor in the Dust

The Immortals

The Soldier's Ghost: A Tale of Charleston

WILLIAM THOMAS
*Runaway Haley:
An Imagined Family Saga*

*The Field of Justice: Moonshine
and Murder in North Georgia*

CLYDE N. WILSON
*Southern Poets and Poems, 1606-1860:
The Land They Loved, Volume 1*

*Confederate Poets and Poems, Vol1
The Land They Loved, Volume II*

Gold-Bug
(Mystery & Suspense Imprint)

BRANDI PERRY
Splintered: A New Orleans Tale

MARTIN WILSON
To Jekyll and Hide